THE LIGHT OF MY LIFE

---∞---

BY JUNE DEVALL

Library of Congress Cataloging-in-Publication Data is available.

ISBN 979-8-89041-573-8

ISBN 979-8-89041-574-5 (for e-book)

THE LIGHT OF MY LIFE

Jesus said,

"I am the light of the world.

He who follows Me shall not walk in darkness,

but have the light of life."

DEDICATION

This book is dedicated to my heavenly Father, who faithfully encouraged me to accept this ultimate challenge, which appeared impossible, and who gently guided me to understand His plan and apply His thoughts that seemed sure and right. I am so thankful for His powerful presence on the journey and the rewarding blessing of knowing my heavenly Father better, loving Him more, and trusting Him completely.

ACKNOWLEDGMENTS

To my granddaughter, Leslie, who took a handwritten
manuscript and transformed it into a typed
and edited copy of this book.

To my son, Bob, who took my verbal vision for the
cover and transformed it into an artistic design
for the contents of this book.

To my daughter, Cindy, who continued to keep me connected
to health care and provided for my wellness to finish this book.

Thank you, special angels, for making a dream a reality.

TABLE OF CONTENTS

Synopsis

The Light of My Life is a collection of stories from the author's century of living. The reader will be inspired by the way beams of treasured truth have been woven through the tapestry of her life that picture proof of God's biblical truth. The reader will be encouraged by the visible rays of His joy and peace in troubling times because they reveal the power of God's presence and His Word to dispel darkness and change lives. The reader who is weary of searching for the meaning of life will discover His answers in the mighty beacons of hope, God's Word, that offers wellness of body, soul, and spirit. Once again, readers of all ages will be amazed by a true miracle from God. He used an ordinary woman, legally blind, in need of assisted living; He led her for two years to hand-write His truth, and then He provided the way and the means to share His love. The wonder of it all is that God initiated His plan when the author was ninety-eight years old! Centuries ago, this awesome God of the Bible promised this miracle.

Even to your old age and gray hairs

I am He, I am He who will sustain you.

I have made you and I will carry you;

I will sustain you and I will rescue you.

Isaiah 46:4 (NIV)

Introduction

"In the beginning,
God created the heavens and the earth.

He saw an empty, shapeless, deep, dark
nothingness!

And He said, 'Let there be light,' and light
was born.

God saw that light was good,
and He separated the light from the darkness."

Genesis 1: 1–5 (paraphrased)

In the beginning, in His first act of creation, the voice of the omnipotent God of the Bible gave birth to light. Because "God is light" (1 John 1:5), and light was His to give. It would be the physical source of life and a constant beam of direction.

In God's creation of physical light, He also foreshadowed a future light He would give from Himself, the very best He could offer. It would be so brilliant and complete that the world would know "God is love" (1 John 4:8). The announcement of this love gift is not only the best-known verse in the Bible, it is the entire Bible in one verse. "For God so loved the world that He gave His only begotten Son, that whoever believes in Him should not perish but have everlasting life" (John 3:16).

This perfect love of God offers the gift of life and light to whoever believes in His Son Jesus, who said, "I am the light of the world."

When I accepted John 3:16 as my personal invitation to believe in Jesus as my Savior and Lord, I began a new life. Part of it included a serious search of His Word for more truth. Throughout the years, these power-packed verses have revealed the magnitude of the awesome God of the Bible that have steadily strengthened my walk with Him. Jesus said, "I am the light of the world. He who follows Me shall not walk in darkness, but have the light of life" (John 8:12). Jesus, in that brilliant and perfect light, promised me sure and steady steps as we walk through together in life.

Believe me, the idea of writing this book did not originate with me! Maybe it was born during the COVID-19 pandemic starting in 2020. The enemy had fired missiles of fear and uncertainty and left society in a state of chaos, confusion, and isolation; "quarantine" was the new law of the land. The shadows of gloom were lifted by rummaging through treasured memories of happiness and writing some related stories. It surprised me how quickly the brightness of joy filtered in. Little did I realize these experiences would become the bedrock God used to launch His new purpose for my life.

With the lifting of some restrictions the following year, I enjoyed resuming Bible studies. At the same time, I began hearing faint whispers to continue reflecting and writing instead of teaching, to begin with the start of my life, and to prepare them for others to read in a binder for family. Even though the whispers were reflective, I did not intend, but I did know that the Lord would walk with me and direct my steps (John 8:12). At age ninety-eight, I accepted His challenge.

As the process evolved, I noticed He had woven a golden thread through the tapestry of all my experiences—each one was a clear picture of some Scriptures. Experience was positive proof of the absolute truth of the Bible! This discovery revealed my purpose: use my stories to share the truth of God's Word and record them in a book.

I have just finished the exciting and rewarding adventure with *The Light of My Life*. It's time for the readers to enjoy the stories and discover for themselves some special truths from He who is the Light of Life, who offers steady beams, joyful rays, and hope-filled beams of light.

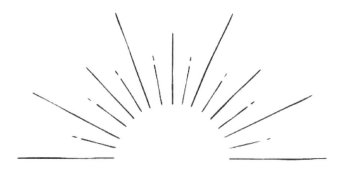

BEAMS OF LIGHT

FROM A

CENTURY OF STORIES

Chapter 1

---∞---

HOME

I heard that the Fourth of July celebration in the windy city of Chicago in 1923 was a spectacular light show of color and design, but it paled in contrast to the celebration held on July 5 in the hearts of Elmer and Elsie. There was no popping of firecrackers or twirling of sparklers, but for sure, there was an explosion of thanksgiving and praise to God for the safe arrival of their firstborn child; "June Girl" was here!

I can't verify their story, but I can testify that growing up in their Christian home gave me the strong foundation I would need to travel my life's journey of faith and confidence in the One who created and delivered me. The first home in which we lived was a city apartment. I remember it as "The Land of I, Me, and Mine," where I reigned for eight years as the "Little Princess." When my little brother made the scene in 1931, I lost my crown, and "sharing lessons" became harder. That same year, my parents followed the trend of living in the suburbs and working in the city and moved to Highland Park on the shores of Lake Michigan. Growing up in this new home was so special. Not only was it saturated with love and laughter, giving me a spiritually healthy pattern to imitate in my home someday, but it packed my treasure chest with vivid memories.

The large house was typical of the period. When entering from the front, you were greeted by a large, enclosed porch from which you entered a foyer. If your path led you straight ahead to the kitchen, you continued circling through a butler's pantry, dining room, living room, and back to the foyer. There, stairs took your feet up to the bedroom and attic or down to the basement. Upstairs, four bedrooms and one bathroom set up their lodging places on the borders of a large foyer. As a youngster, my concern was that the door to the storage attic was in my bedroom! Not knowing what "spooky" thing could be lurking up there, I made sure a chair guarded that door. The basement was unique. There was so much to see. The boss of that place was the huge black furnace set in the middle of the space. His long arms reached up to hidden holes through which he shoved his hot breath to keep you warm on freezing days. Our comfort came at a high cost. His hunger pains required many shovels of coal many times a day. The coal bin was well stocked! And so was our food cellar closet. Lots of labeled jars with home-canned fruits and vegetables were ready for choosing at a later time. Anything that broke got fixed at Dad's organized workbench and test center. Another corner held Mom's laundry center for Monday's project (the day I made us pancakes when I came home from school for lunch). A portable washing machine, two huge rinsing tubs, and a metal table made the furnishings. The electric train and village set up on the ping-pong table was Dad's pride and joy. Yes, all grown men have toys! The long backyard was framed by flowering lilac bushes on one side and a single-car garage on the other. Both sides were determined to protect the beauty of what lived within the vegetable garden and flower beds.

The sweetest memories, though, are the ones built on family relationships. The best-remembered ones seemed to fall into two categories: me-centered or parent-centered. Take Sunday afternoon, for example. It was a jam-packed, fun-filled, rip-roaring time when city relatives came to visit. They loved the scenic drive to the suburbs to catch up on weekly news and then fill up on a light German supper of juicy hot dogs, hot potato salad, and perfect cheesecake. During the "news" session, the aunts and uncles voiced their loud opinions about everything. In between statements would come loud bursts of homemade humor. To this soundboard of noise, the cousins around the monopoly table added their squeals and shouts until it was time to get rid of pent-up energy in backyard games. Sunday mornings were definitely parent-centered, especially during my teens when worldly interests were more exciting than going to church. When my dad said it was time to get up, you can't imagine how many excuses I tried to stay home, but not one ever worked. His motivational statement was always the same: "You'll feel better after going to church. If not, you can stay in bed all afternoon and be well to go to school tomorrow." Riding to church, I thought my dad was wiser than Solomon.

Since my mom's expertise blossomed in art and music, she monitored my daily practicing at the piano, that is, until her aspirations for developing a concert pianist vanished. Also, she was more lenient than Dad when it came to time. If I was running a little late after a date, I could always count on her playing the radio in the kitchen to dull the sound of squeaky stairs, and I quickly slipped up to my room. And yes, we prayed that sweet man to be laying on his good ear!

I'm sure there's a verse in the Bible that says something about "cleanliness is a trademark virtue of godliness." Everything in our house had to be squeaky clean. Everything took its turn, from curtains and carpets to walls and windows. Wallpaper cleaning day was fun to watch. Dad used a ladder to reach the top part of the wall and a drop cloth to catch the falling dirt crumbles that fell when huge erasers were dragged down the wall. Mom would clean the lower sections of the wall. It was amazing how sleepy colors woke up so fast.

Food played a leading role in our home. I looked forward to the sweet aroma drifting from the kitchen to greet me after school; there were cookies for munching and coffee cake for breakfast slicing. After a day in the city, Dad would relish our special family time around the supper table, where Mom's tasty meal took center stage. Her choice cut of meat laid the foundation for the two sides of white potato and a vegetable. Bread and real butter were always present, as was that delicious dessert. I knew Mom could have won a bundle of blue ribbons for her recipes in any contest.

Even though there are merely a century of memories in my treasure chest, today's rummaging seemed to focus on that home into which Elmer and Elsie moved their young family in 1931. My brother and I received a bountiful harvest of blessings because our parents believed and trusted in God's Word. They knew the truth recorded by King Solomon in Proverbs 22:6, "Train up a child in the way he should go, and when he is old he will not depart from it," and in Psalm 127:1 (NIV), "Unless the Lord builds the house, they labor in vain who build it." Jesus voiced the same truth in His sermon on the mount in Matthew 7:24–25: No storm can destroy a house that is built on the rock. God is the foundation; He "blesses the home of the righteous" (Proverbs 3:33, NIV). I am so grateful for God-loving parents who could say, "in Him we live and move and have our being" (Acts 17:28).

Chapter 2

---◦◦◦---

GRANDPARENTS

It must be "Grandparents Day" and time to sift through memorable stories from my amazing grandparents, who had a magical way of turning everyday events into bright and happy moments. Do you think it was the longevity that gave birth to their great wisdom to say the right words or do the best things at any given time? I'm inclined to believe they knew the true source of all life who gives insight to be and do what pleases Him and could say with the psalmist, "The Lord is my light" (Psalm 27:1).

Let's begin with some snapshots of Mom's side of the family, Grandpa Emil and Grandma Pauline. Most of Grandpa's are faded because I was four when he died, but one is very clear. This tall man with sparkling blue eyes had a strong, authoritative voice that still echoes from the supper table, "If Mama cooked it, it's good. We eat everything on our plate." It didn't matter if eating added extra pounds to the body; no food could be wasted. This was a typical message spoken by all industrious Germans who migrated to America, the land of opportunity. On the other hand, the mind pictures of Grandma Pauline are in abundance and still so vivid.

My favorite ones were the exciting holiday parties in her big house; whether we gathered in the front living room dominated by the grand piano or in the back dining room that featured a banquet-sized table, twenty-two active bodies found chairs before filling the air with a chorus of hearty laughter. Gift-giving and fancy-food-eating were important, but the Children's Production was the highlight. Each of the eleven grandchildren took a turn to display their talent at the piano or near the piano to sing or recite a poem or story. At the end of each rendition, Grandma would hug and praise the performer in such a special way that each one believed that he or she was Grandma's favorite true love.

As I grew up, I especially enjoyed listening to her review the events of her life, ordinary things that were colored by joy or sorrow and success or failure. She had an abundance of stories that bubbled up from her wellspring of longevity. One was of her journey to America at age sixteen with her older sister as her only companion, the hardships of traveling in steerage on the steamer for many weeks, and the embarrassment of having her name and her destination stitched in the pocket of her apron because she couldn't speak English. This was my first glimpse of a very strong woman. When she was twenty-two and Grandpa was thirty, they married and settled in a German community in Chicago's north side. The next fourteen years seemed overwhelming to me, but they viewed them as life and took them in stride: the birth of their ten children, the death of five children, and establishing and operating a successful bakery—all at the same time! I don't know when they found time to visit with their friends across the street who lived above their butcher shop, the Oscar Mayer family. These industrious merchants met their challenges with hard work and perseverance and demonstrated that America was truly the land of opportunity in which to succeed. Grandpa was no exception. Over the years, his nest egg grew, and he was able to venture out into buying and selling apartment buildings; the profits provided Grandma with a very comfortable life for her thirty-four years of widowhood. Reflecting upon the priceless tales told so many years ago has deepened my appreciation for the pillar of a lady I called "Grandma" instilled a fresh pride in my German heritage, and impressed me to continue this important storytelling tradition. Linking the generations of the family, their dreams, and their struggles is a worthy task that must be preserved. God admonishes us to do the same thing in His family. When we know Him and have experienced His perfect love, we also have been commissioned to pass it on to the next generation. The psalmist tells us, "Listen to what our fathers have told us and not hide it from the children. Tell the generations to come the praises of the Lord" (Psalm 78:4, paraphrased). This was the special blessing I received from Grandpa Benjamin, my dad's father. He was a preacher who "walked his talk." By weaving the Word of God into the aspects of daily living, he painted for me many memorable pictures of a loving God. Even though he was strict, he was fun to be with. When I misbehaved and needed his correction, I knew he would follow it with his big bear hugs and encouraging words. It was his way of covering the sting of discipline with the necessary warm blanket of forgiving love.

Music played an integral part in Grandpa Benjamin's and Grandma Ricki's home. If Grandma was at the piano, Grandpa was blowing his trumpet or beating his drums. If he was tickling the keys, she was leading the singing. The gathering may have been smaller than the one at Grandma Pauline's, but it certainly exceeded in gusto and tempo. God's folks were not "laid back"; they were always on the move. I believe my dad and I learned the two-step from Grandpa Benjamin: ascending and descending the stairs two steps at a time!

From Grandma Ricki's stories, I knew hard work, long hours, and few material possessions were her challenges of being a preacher's wife and mother of four children. The church gave them a parsonage in which to live, plenty of fresh eggs and chickens to eat, and a few dollars to spend. This meager income was supplemented by the contents of their garden. I don't know when she found time to put up their delicious peaches that we enjoyed so much or to have a pitcher of ice-cold freshly squeezed lemonade ready whenever we visited. Those two tastes will always remind me of my happy, God-loving grandma.

Personally, I do not know anyone other than Grandma Ricki who had this experience when leaving this life—she died *twice* within a week! The first time was expected; she was sick. But even though expected, the reality caused her daughter to scream, "Mama, don't leave us!" Several minutes after the doctor pronounced her passing, her eyelids fluttered, and her mouth framed words. Then, slowly, she spoke, "Heaven is beautiful. I didn't want to leave. Never stop me again." Grandma had seen the Holy City! Before that, she had believed the truth of Revelation 21 recorded by the apostle John: "The Holy City was like a bride adorned for her husband" (Revelation 21:2), "great, high walls with twelve gates" (Revelation 21:12), "each gate made from one pearl" (Revelation 21:21), "twelve foundations of wall each adorned with precious stones" (Revelation 21:19), "streets of pure gold like transparent glass" (Revelation 21:21), and "the city was illuminated by God's glory, the Lamb of God" (Revelation 21:23). One week later, her wishes were honored and angels escorted her through those pearly gates. I don't know why Grandma was allowed that glimpse of glory. Maybe it was a special reward for her faith in God, believing the truth of His Word before she saw her heavenly home.

"Grandparents Day" has ended; the sifting of memories is finished for today. Before I close the lid of this golden chest, I'll slip in this note to these precious people.

"Thank you for being in my life. You were essential in those early years when I wore 'rose-colored glasses' and danced through the land of 'Me and Mine.' You were never too busy to play a new game, sing a silly little song, or snuggle together with an exciting old story. You were essential during those terrifying teens. When anything could ignite a crisis and shatter my world, you had the knack to say the words to extinguish the flames and restore a calm spirit. You were essential when adulthood made the scene, and the world would whisper her alluring ways. With cautious advice, your wise words strengthened my family-taught spiritual values. Thank you for smoothing my transition from fantasyland to the real world of reality and your sun-kissed love that brightened the journey."

Chapter 3

My True Love

Sometime during my high school years, I discovered the thrill of a flirtatious wink or a secretly passed note from that handsome boy across the room that initiated my search for "Mr. One-and-Only." By graduation, I had a plan that would unfold on a college campus; I would join a sorority where social activities were unlimited. Because my dad's purpose for higher education was slightly different, I selected a school with stellar academic routines, Northwestern University in Evanston, Illinois. He was pleased with my choice, and I was pleased with the smooth progress of my plan. And then, so suddenly, it hit a brick wall when the word "schedule" came up in what began as a simple conversation one day.

Dad: "Have you made out your schedule yet?"

Me: "No, but I will."

Dad: "The North Shore line offers a wide range of departures and returns."

Me: "What does a train schedule have to do with my going to college?"

Dad: "You will know how early to leave home each day to make your early morning classes."

Me: "I'm not commuting; I'm living in the dorm!"

Dad: "If I pay for your college, you will live at home and take the train each day, only thirty minutes there."

Me: "I'm not going to college that way!"

Dad: "That's up to you. If you don't go to school, you'll have to get a job to pay for room and board."

Me: "Well, that's exactly what I'll do! I'll go to work!"

Hindsight is an excellent teacher. Looking back on the complete collapse of my perfect plan for finding "Mr. Right," I learned God had a better idea. His Word says, "I know the good plans I have for you to give you a future and a hope" (Jeremiah 29:11, paraphrased). Time revealed it would not be at a college in Evanston on a campus near a sorority; it would be at a Midshipmen's School in Chicago on Michigan Avenue near my job! It took eighteen months for the reality of that truth.

After Japan launched its sinister attack on Pearl Harbor, Honolulu, on December 7, 1941, World War II was declared, convincing many young naval recruits to apply for officer training at a Midshipmen's School. Those who entered and earned degrees left as Ensigns for new assignments. Their school schedules always provided time for recreation, so dates were plentiful. But by the second week in June 1943, I knew God had finalized His plan for me. His match-made-in-heaven was off to a racing start!

Do you remember at age nineteen, the big Saturday date gets canceled, and you have to choose between boredom at home or disappointment on a blind date? I opted for a blind date on a double date, provided I got a sneak peek. The plan was simple. My cousin's boyfriend from Midshipmen's School would bring his roommate to the after-work hangout where everyone went to meet someone for a drink. I sat with a clear view of the door to see the two men. The one I knew; the other *I had to know*!

That first date for dinner, dancing, and conversation with Les DeVall in June 1943 was pure magic; it beautifully framed our sixty-five-year marriage. In those eight spellbinding hours, my heart was completely captivated by this man of God; I knew he was God's man for me. During our four-month whirlwind courtship, we were inseparable. After work, we spent time in the city sharing treasured thoughts. On weekends, we spent our hours in Highland Park, where Les was quickly earning gold medals from his future family. It was ironic that mom's front porch sleeping sofa, Les's nighttime buddy, was inherited by our clan four decades later. Today, it faithfully provides quality naps for my grandson's family.

On Saturday night, October 30, 1943, our families and friends rejoiced as my true love and I committed our lives to each other in a simple church wedding. Les and his best man were handsome in their Ensign uniforms. My maid of honor and I were beaming as we walked down the aisle in our new Sunday dresses and hats. The soloist was inspiring as she sang our songs with her angelic voice, and our preacher was so joyful as he joined two hearts, soul mates for eternity. Our marriage would be living proof of God's truth, "what God has joined together will be inseparable" (Matthew 19: 5–6, paraphrased).

A bitterly cold, dark winter storm raged outside God's church, but the warm light of His love blazed within.

Chapter 4

The World of Reality

Chicago was beyond amazing in showing its appreciation to American servicemen during World War II, especially in the last two years. The city gave them free tickets to sporting events, museums, movies, concerts, and stage shows; free passes on public transportation within the city; and many dining discounts to established eateries. After a workday, we would explore the area's nightlife. On weekends, we toured the other sites or would go home to see Mom and Dad. For sure, we were caught up in an exciting whirlwind of non-stop, pleasurable experiences. Ensign pay plus my paycheck, coupled with the city's free gifts, gave us a great sense of freedom from financial concerns. Les's Pacific duty at the beginning of the war lowered the possibility of our being separated by another overseas assignment, especially with the new promotion to one of the school's Company Commanders. And then, the icing on the cake was the thrilling news of "love multiplication"; our first baby would arrive in February 1945! Absolutely, life was too wonderful for words!

My pregnancy was a real game-changer. From fast and furious, we became more relaxed and definitely moved at a slower pace. My priorities made a gradual shift from self-centered to a genuine focus on someone else's interest. The temporal things offered by the world's system began to fade; they were being trumped by the eternal values I learned as a child. Life was taking on a new soft glow; life was anew wonderful!

Before Thanksgiving, when our lease was up, we accepted the invitation from my parents to move home for a few months so they could help with the baby. They knew I would need time to recoup and lessons to cope with the scary moments in untraveled waters. Believe me, I basked in the sunshine and warmth of their loving attention as these two angels turned their precious days of waiting into a perfect season of beauty. I knew Mom and Dad's TLC would magnify as we welcomed our baby.

It appeared so suddenly, without any warning or a single sign. A tempestuous black storm assaulted the light of God's love, slammed our lives, and ripped open our hearts. Death had kicked open the doors of our sanctuary and stole our first-born son!

But the God of all comfort was present! He saw the devastation. With His love and gentleness, He picked up the broken pieces; He fashioned them securely. It would be all for His purpose and in His time. The beauty of the reality of God that emerged from heartache was God-designed. He used the sorrow He had allowed to become the strong magnet to initiate a meaningful relationship with Him, to really know Him, rather than just about Him. In this classroom of life, God's curriculum is not easy, and there is no graduation day. But with my desire and diligence, I experienced rewards beyond belief. In time, I learned that the better I knew Him, the greater I could trust Him. This led to living with pure joy and purpose, even in the heavy trials and tribulations. The abundant life was becoming the new normal.

The words of truth in the Bible are an arsenal of weapons to fight the fears and anxieties when trials and tribulations make the scene. They will dispel any darkness with their encouraging rays of sunshine.

The words of the prophet Isaiah will lift and carry a burdensome soul through the darkest storm, an encounter that will renew strength for the next squall on the horizon. "When you pass through the waters, I will be with you; and through the rivers, they shall not overflow you. When you walk through the fire, you shall not be burned, nor shall the flame scorch you" (Isaiah 43:2).

Because of God's unlimited love for His children, He will use all of their circumstances and experiences to mold them for their purpose. In his letter to the Christians in Rome, the apostle Paul recorded so succinctly this encouraging truth. "And we know that in all things God works for the good of those who love him, who have been called according to his purpose" (Romans 8:28, NIV).

I have learned that God is real; He is faithful to His Word. The Bible is true, all of it. The Scriptures are powerful, encouraging, and transformative. They are beacons of bright light, absolutely essential to discern the best paths to take in the world of reality without those old rose-colored glasses.

Chapter 5

SEASONS OF CHANGE

Would you agree that comfort is high on the list of lifestyles for most Americans? If you enjoy wearing loose clothing that the dryer didn't shrink, sitting on padded church pews, relaxing to favorite tunes under the soothing hum of the ceiling fan, or frequently feeding your body sweet goodies, then you have cast a positive vote. Most of us are prone to root out our special space, line it with comfortable touches, and then hang out the "Do Not Disturb" sign. But honesty warns that a life without stimulating encounters leads to atrophy. Though not always pleasant or desirable, challenges are needed for our entire well-being.

In reflecting upon nearly a century of these life-molding changes, I realized that they had fortified the truth of God's Word, and it is in God's Word; "All Scripture is given by inspiration of God" (2 Timothy 3:16), and Jesus, the son of God said, "Your word is truth" (John 17:17). One verse, in particular, has been engraved into my mind as true, "I am sure that God does take all of our experiences and circumstances and He does work them together for the good of His children" (Romans 8:28, paraphrased). When World War II ended in the summer of 1945, changes in my life began with racing speed.

Before Les settled into his new job in Chicago, we planned a short visit to Mississippi to see his family. Surprisingly, it included a chance meeting with his former football coach, who posed one question that changed our lives completely, "Would you join my football staff this season at Hinds Junior College in Raymond?" Because of his love of the game, great ability on the playing field, and his life's dream to coach, we both knew his only answer had to be a resounding "Yes!" Immediately, a permanent move from North to South had replaced a short visit from North to South and back again! Time did not permit necessary farewells or closure on all that was familiar and secure. The move from Chicago to Raymond in August 1945 was traumatic! But God... He used it and my experiences of the six-and-a-half years that followed to bless me with His greatest gift!

My first year in the South was hard. Even before daybreak, the heat and humidity showed no mercy; all comfort had been shoved in some hidden closet. Without any energy, survival was questionable.

Room and board on the campus was part of the pay package, but when I saw our apartment at the back of a noisy boys' dorm, the thought of living there was doubtful. What was to be a "happy home" to humans was already occupied by a colony of lively roaches! An excessive number of bug bombs were called in to evict them.

Communication was a major hurdle. I was lost in trying to decipher the meanings of the sounds I heard, words that were stretched out, heavy with dialect, and speech loaded with idioms. Les was my great translator while I learned the "language."

Eating in the faculty dining room three times a day was not only a language classroom but also a learning lab for trying different foods. One day, in particular, was very different. I heard it was "stew" but did not ask why the gravy was white instead of brown until after I enjoyed my meal. When I heard, "It was *rabbit* stew," I received a miracle: I did not faint! The people at our table were even more astonished; they had just seen a Yankee eat and enjoy one of their favorite meals.

Les was so busy coaching or teaching or preparing to teach that his time with me seemed limited to "meal dates." Time hung heavy with nothing to do, even if I had any energy. Empty hours quickly became the prime motivator for pursuing a college degree majoring in Business Education. Little did I know then that this "time thing" was God's divine plan to guide my steps on His path for my life.

Seeing the town of Raymond for the first time was another "I can't believe this" experience! The memory of this transplanted city girl is still vivid; the tour is not lengthy. The hub consisted of a water tower encircled by a grocery store, general merchandise business, doctor's office/pharmacy, post office, car dealership/service station, and café. A few roads extended out and led to the churches and schools and a stately old courthouse. That day, I could not have imagined, not in my wildest dreams, that I would actually miss that quaint town or be heartsick about moving away from those dear people who lovingly helped me to receive God's greatest gift.

After a year of major adjustments to Southern living, I was no longer a stranger dwelling in a foreign land. By then, we had taken God seriously when He told man, "Be fruitful and multiply" (Genesis 1:28), and we were ecstatic to learn of my pregnancy. Young and naive, we were totally unaware of the new challenges that accompanied having babies and building families.

Separation from comfort returned in August 1946 with the arrival of our precious baby girl, whom we nicknamed Cindy. Les called her his little "cheerleader" and that she became, with pride, an admiration for her "coach" and a special love for her daddy. The beginning of her life was hard for all of us. Finding her correct formula and establishing some type of sleeping schedule took many months and much patience, but the rewards were great; food and sleep dispelled anxieties and stress!

By the time little Bobby signed the family register in December 1948, we were living in a faculty house with more space and a backyard that bordered some woods. It didn't take long to switch to high gear to keep track of the "mover." At nine months, he had perfected his escape from the playpen. Around fifteen months, he fell off the porch and split his tongue, which required emergency surgery by his dad! Around the age of two, his toes in the flower trellis took him to the roof to "see the woods"! An SOS call to Mom brought her experienced touch and encouraging words and left us with the assurance that all of us would survive. The Bible tells us that there are angels in heaven assigned to watch over the children (Matthew 18:10, paraphrased), but I knew one who lived here on Earth.

In August 1951, our baby Diane made her debut to complete our God-given family. I believe her happy adjustment to the new world was due to two things. Because I had thrown away the book on raising newborns, she was on her own schedule of eating and sleeping. Also, for nine months, she had been listening to her mama tell her she had to be good or she would be sent back to where she came from! She was a keen observer of the behavior—and its consequences—of her siblings and learned what to avoid. Raising Diane was not hard; what was difficult was the time spent in the hospital after delivery before going home. That experience proved to be essential! When I regained consciousness three days after the delivery, I wondered why so many somber faces with hollow eyes were peering at me. What was wrong? Les had just told me we had another healthy little girl; the two at home were in good hands. The tubes in my mouth prevented any questions. Then, gradually, Les began to fill in the events of the three-day nightmare. Complications had developed after delivery, doctors were unable to stop the hemorrhaging, my death was certain without surgery, and survival of that ordeal was very doubtful. To that bleak diagnosis, he answered decisively, "If she's going to die anyway, then *operate*! *Try* to save her!"

The great physician heard Les's plea and fervent prayers. Just as surely as dawn chases away each midnight's dark watch, the light of God's love banished despair with His promise of hope for a complete healing.

Once again, God's Word proved to be true. In the Old Testament, the prophet Jeremiah recorded God's admonition to use his "phone number," "Call to Me, and I will answer you, and show you great and mighty things, which you do not know" (Jeremiah 33:3). In the New Testament, James tells us to "persevere with fervent prayers and experience God's great deeds" (James 5:16, paraphrased). Be strengthened by the rays of sunshine; dawn always follows each night.

Complete healing of my body came, along with a fresh awareness of God's love for me. A serious introspection was initiated by an innocent question from our young child who asked, "Why does our family go to two churches?" Cindy was referring to "Daddy's church" and "Mommy's church." I did not have an answer for her. I did not have an answer for any of life's important questions; I did not really know the One who is the answer for life. Once again, God sent His angels to me, this time in the form of loving hearts from "Daddy's church." They explained the meanings of these Scriptures I had memorized as a child so long ago. And with understanding, a response was demanded: a giant step of faith!

In that sleepy little town of Raymond, at the age of twenty-eight, I asked Jesus to forgive me of my sins and dwell with me as my personal Lord and Savior. It was then that I became a Christian; then, my name was written in God's book of eternal life; and then, I began the journey of the abundant life Jesus promised, "I have come that they may have life, and that they may have it more abundantly" (John 10:10). That full and satisfying life began immediately with a job at "our" church. Being the secretary to the new young and enthusiastic preacher was not a job! It was a daily feast at the Lord's banquet table. It was everything I needed to grow as a Christian those last two years we remained at this college. After nearly a decade of challenging changes, it was God's loving reward to begin our amazing relationship as we moved on to new adventures.

Steel and Velvet

His light He ordered, black depths to pierce;
Split-seas in heaven, their limits He set;
By His command, all earth bore life;
For signs and times, His lights He hung.
The words of the King were strong and bold;
His flawless world was richly born.
This awesome realm, a ruler it lacked.
A man He shaped, His breath He gave;
This image of God would reign with love
That mighty one? I knew him not.

A choice He gave this man He made;
His Maker to serve or himself to please?
Man wished to obey but His will was weak;
The selfish life he quickly chose.
The heart of the Father was tender and full
With love and forgiveness for a sinful soul.
Man's curse was death, so His Son He sent;
His blood He shed, man's debt He paid!
God's gift of grace? It's free for all.
This loving one? I know him well.

June DeVall
March 25, 1999

Chapter 6

---⸎---

ABSOLUTELY IMPOSSIBLE

Life was ideal and secure. My relationship with God was maturing, our marriage was sweeter than ever, and the children were healthy, with sibling rivalries a minor issue. Les's football coaching career was widely recognized by his winning seasons; being Pastor John's secretary was greatly inspiring; and, along with the church family, our involvement in God's service was very rewarding. Our roots in Raymond were firmly planted, and our "Happy Family" flag flew high over our home sweet home.

Do you remember reading about *the move* (1945) that ushered in my "season of change"? Because history has a tendency to repeat itself, you'll understand that new, undesired challenges are bound to evolve from *the call* as well!

One day in early January 1954, Les received a phone call from a stranger in Hattiesburg, Mississippi. He identified himself as the president of Mississippi Women's College. Because their enrollment was down to a hundred students, they were in jeopardy of closing and needed revitalization. And then he made the most absurd, utterly ridiculous statement imaginable, "God said you are to come here and establish a men's complete athletic program of football, basketball, baseball, and track, starting with football this fall." We sensed these were words from a desperate man grasping a straw to save his school. God wouldn't say that! Or would He?

After four stressful months of intense soul-searching, fervently praying for godly wisdom, weekly conversations with God's message, and daily struggling between will and our comfort zone, we were convicted to trust God completely. We took down our "Happy Family" flag and, along with the three children, packed it in the old green Chevy to head off to meet our new scary but exciting season of challenging changes.

The logistics of anyone fielding a neophyte football team within three months was overwhelming! But this was God's plan, and He does not lie (Psalm 89:35). By trusting in God when He said, "With men this is impossible, but with God all things are possible" (Matthew 19:26), Les was used by God to make everything happen.

Capable players with the courage to try the untried and the stamina to work out in grueling August heat were recruited. A ten-game schedule with reputable teams was completed. The University of Southern Mississippi's stadium across town was used for home games. And money was raised to fund the essential needs of this new unbudgeted sport. God's mission was accomplished!

The inauguration of a men's athletic program gave birth to a coeducational William Carey College in 1954. After two winning seasons, the less costly sport of basketball replaced football as the drawing card for the increasing enrollment period. In 2006, the college became William Carey University, with today's enrollment of over 4000! Who could ever doubt the truth that nothing is impossible for the awesome God of the Holy Bible?

Chapter 7

New Beginnings

After the great joy of being used by God as He gave birth to William Carey College, our clan of five, plus Missy and her new litter of Cocker Spaniel puppies, decided to make Louisiana our permanent home and fly our "Happy Family" flag. That transition became the new beginning that changed my life.

During the one-year stop at Louisiana College in Pineville, both Les and I achieved a personal goal. He successfully entered the arena of football coaches in the Gulf States Conference, and I completed the college curriculum to earn a BS degree in Business Education with certification to teach. The timing was perfect for Les to accept our new challenge to build a football program at McNeese State University in Lake Charles.

On June 27, 1957, just three weeks after moving into our home, we were "welcomed" to the state by an unexpected, unannounced, ugly creature named Audrey! At 5:00 a.m., she began pounding on our windows and doors, screeched deadly threats, and slapped the roof of its chipped white marble before snapping the power lines. Then, with enraged fury, she gave wings to sturdy brick fences and securely rooted trees, all before her complete collapse from sheer exhaustion.

Even though Hurricane Audrey took out her wrath on the things of this world, God's Word was our shield of defense, our light in this darkness. To the prophet Isaiah, He said, "When you pass through the waters, I *will be* with you; and through the rivers, they shall not overflow you. When you walk through the fire, you shall not be burned, nor shall the flame scorch you" (Isaiah 43:2). In another passage He said, "Fear not, for

I *am* with you; be not dismayed, for I *am* your God. I will strengthen you, yes, I will help you, I will uphold you with My righteous right hand" (Isaiah 41:10).

The hurricane was over, things got fixed, and now it was time to begin again, to let the newness of living and working in Lake Charles become our focus. Before long, we had found our new church home and had begun meeting some members of our new spiritual family. Les became director of the College and Career Development, in which both of us taught Sunday Bible lessons. The children were enrolled in the same neighborhood school, one of the best in the parish, with high academic standards and gifted teachers. Everyone was thrilled that our subdivision was running over with young families and children. Our neighbors were never too busy mowing to stop and share a few words with the "newcomers." Because all the children would be in school, I wanted to begin my teaching career and was so grateful to sign my first contract, especially when I learned I would be working in the city's best junior high. Since Les would be working at McNeese, I was excited about attending a wide variety of activities with the faculty.

The move to Lake Charles proved to be a significant one. Les successfully met—and exceeded—his challenge by giving McNeese all winning seasons and four Gulf States Championships! After that nine-year record, he retired from coaching to serve there as an administrator until full retirement in 1980. He needed to devote some serious time to some serious fishing at our place at Toledo Bend Lake. He knew where the "honey holes" were and was determined to find the quality bass, brim, and white perch. And who knew, maybe lucky enough to hook a real winner to mount! And yes, he continued to set goals, achieve challenges, and break records while seriously fishing up in Pirates Cove. I truly believe those relaxing days with their fun-filled challenges were a special love gift from the Father to His child.

For me, our move to Lake Charles became the open door to the greatest "New Beginning" of my life!

I was excited to begin teaching, and the balancing of work with family responsibilities was going smoothly. That early morning hour with God was so special, the source of my strength and direction for the day. Our social life was rich to me: it centered around the church family with a full calendar of activities in homes as well as at church. When McNeese opened in the fall, invitations to their events and to parties with the new faculty friends were highlighted social activities. Along with them came the ones from my faculty. I don't remember when, but before long, a very worthy civic organization was begging for help. I could not refuse, and there was an empty board chair.

Reflecting back on that first decade in Lake Charles, I realized that my time "doing with people" had surpassed my time of "being with God." The shift had been so gradual, so subtle, that it was hardly noticed except by the Great Physician. His diagnosis was correct; my business with "things" was the thief that had stolen my stamina and robbed me of my joy.

To the psalmist, God gave His sure cure for this sickness: "Be still and know that I am God" (Psalm 46:10). Specific instructions for complete healing were recorded by the prophet

Isaiah: "For thus says the Lord God, the Holy One of Israel: 'In returning and rest you shall be saved; in quietness and confidence shall be your strength'" (Isaiah 30:15). The meaning was clear. If I desired a restored relationship with the Lord God, He would be number one, not others. My responsibility was to submit my will to His perfect will by confessing this sin to Him and then, by resting in this Holy One to handle things, to trust in Him completely. It was time for a "New Beginning".

It was in the mid-1970s, some twenty years after Jesus became my Savior, that I took a giant leap of faith. I asked Jesus to be the Lord of my life, one that was surrendered to Him and committed to trusting Him in and with all things. The lordship of Jesus was aptly described by King Solomon, who said, "Trust in the Lord with all your heart, and lean not on your own understanding; in all your ways acknowledge Him, and He shall direct your paths. Do not be wise in your own eyes; fear the Lord and depart from evil" (Proverbs 3:5–7).

This new segment of life's journey began with a declaration, a desire for lordship. But for this transformation to become a reality, time would be needed to retrain a strong self-will to abdicate the throne. I was to conduct these sessions with daily, in-depth studies of God's Word, followed by pensive reflection on their truths. No lesson was complete without quiet conversations with God to gain His wisdom for application. And yes, I am still monitoring those daily sessions; there is no graduation class!

Today, when my unruly will attempts a show of strength, I quickly head to my prayer chair. After thanking God for

His incredible patience with me, I immediately follow the apostle John's wise advice to get back on the forward path: "If we confess our sins, He is faithful and just to forgive us our sins and to cleanse us from all unrighteousness" (1 John 1:9). I claim this promise often. I have learned that confession is my healing lotion for the sores of sin. The opportunity to begin again, over and over, is the rich blessing that follows confession!

Jesus promised us that by traveling with Him, we will experience the "abundant life" in His presence (John 10:10). His promise is true. Once I experienced His unspeakable joy and unbelievable peace, I knew I could live no other way.

I think I'll end my reflection today with some holy advice from the wisest man who ever lived, King Solomon. Even though he penned it some 3,000 years ago, it's good today. Trust is the open door to living an abundant life.

Oh, taste and see that the Lord is good,

blessed is the man who trusts in Him!

Psalm 34:8

Chapter 8

---⚬⚬⚬---

Retired?

On one hot afternoon in May of 1984, I turned off the AC in my classroom, knowing that it would be the last time. The large wooden cabinet that contained teaching supplies and textbooks had been purged of non-essentials to display neatly stacked books; the metal filing drawers of treasured stories, poems, games, and puzzles for enrichment activities had been reorganized by units to help the new incoming teacher; bulletin boards had been stripped and ready for fresh ideas for the next class; and the empty desk held only a few pens and a pad of paper. After nearly three decades of teaching, closing the door behind me was a bittersweet moment of leaving behind and looking ahead.

With three weeks of unwinding under my belt, the back porch called my name to sip a second cup of coffee while savoring beauty's display of design and color that covered the yard. Only some small talk by chattering birds disturbed the silence of peace. The setting was perfect for reflecting once again on our family's bountiful blessings. With the good minds God had given them, the children had earned both their bachelor's and master's degrees to teach, coach, and counsel in high school. Cindy chose to be single, Bob was divorced, a father to a young son, and Diane was married to a medical doctor and "Mom" to their three children. Wherever their paths led, God walked with them; His presence was their strength and joy. As for my true love and me, He filled our empty nest with a new season of sweetness.

My state of bliss shifted into action when I picked up the morning paper to scan the headlines. At the bottom of the first page was a question that caught my attention and gave birth to an exciting few years of my retirement. "Do you enjoy doing needlecraft and being with people? Call Cathy..." I knew God had surprised me with an open door to teach my favorite hobby to other women and, at the same time, to be rewarded with new, lasting friendships. Ongoing benefits were the abundance of free materials to stitch and lucrative paychecks to deposit! Cathy had gone over the basics of training new reps. They included getting ways to obtain leads for home parties, what to cover with the hostess for a successful party with great sales and many personal gifts, tips for recruiting new reps at parties, and how to handle the business of direct sales. When Cathy finished, I knew that this new adventure in needlecraft was for me. What I did not know then was the rest of what God had in mind for me to do besides teach ladies how to stitch. Reflecting on those seven delightful years, I believe He had a greater purpose than giving me a fun outlet for my hobby. Over the years, strong friendships developed into opportunities to "teach" them the Good News of God's love for them; that was my greatest blessing. Later, I will share the life-changing story of my very first hostess.

God told the prophet Jeremiah that even before he was born, He knew the good plans He had for him (Jeremiah 29:11). King David praised the Lord for His incredible knowledge. David said that before any were born, God knew his sitting down and rising up, his ways and thoughts, and all the words of his tongue (Psalm 139:2–4). Such knowledge is too wonderful for me; it is high, I cannot attain it" (Psalm 139:6). God's complete knowledge (omniscience) is an attribute no mortal being can ever possess. I'm so thankful God knew His good plan for me to accomplish His good purpose through me.

Retirement from the public educational system in 1984 not only sparked an exciting new career from a hobby but also introduced me to a unique organization of Christian women who shared God's love with women whose hearts were hungry to know Him. I had learned of the career in direct sales through a question in the newspaper by a stranger named Cathy; and the Christian Women's Club (CWC) through a conversation at a basketball game by a stranger named Kelly.

Three months before beginning in direct sales, Les and I were sitting in the stands at a McNeese game when a friendly couple took the empty seats next to us. The two men knew each other, so small talk flowed freely. Realizing that Kelly and I would continue to talk during the game, two seats were exchanged so the men could watch the game. Conversation with Kelly was so easy and relaxed that it made time take wings. At the end of the game, we left with an invitation to be their guests at Christian Women's annual Guest Night Dinner at the country club in a few weeks. But more importantly, I left the game knowing that a magical bond had been sealed that night, one that developed into a precious friendship over the years. After attending the Guest Night dinner party, I knew that the Christian Women's Club had already taken root in my life, and after the first ladies' luncheon in June 1984, I was certain that involvement in CWC would become my priority service to God. A gracious hostess welcomed me with the warmth of my best friend. Her partner followed suit as she led me to the name tag table. Once pinned, my name tag became a magnet for more "old friends" to greet and assist me in picking up my ticket. From there, I had a personal escort to a selected table; my table hostess was a pro! With so much ease, she kept everyone at her table connected during the entire luncheon.

The first hour was festive, completely saturated with fun and laughter. While we ate a delicious meal, we were entertained by the soloist's lively secular song and then a dreamy style show (the special feature that month). In between the various activities, a variety of gift-giving added more sparkle to the party. The happy party atmosphere was a unique prelude to introducing the ladies to the joy of experiencing the love of God. This smooth transition to a more serious tone was made through the musician's sacred song. The music opened our hearts to receive the inspiring testimony of the speaker's walk with God. Truly, her message was the highlight of the luncheon. When I left that day, wrapped up in all those warm hugs and big smiles, I agreed with my joy-filled spirit that I had found the spiritual niche where I belonged. During the thirty years following that luncheon, my primary focus was working with the ladies on their planning team. This well-organized group consisted of a chairman and many coordinators, each with specific responsibilities for a segment of the total program. These devoted women earmarked the first three Wednesdays of every month for planning, prayer coffees, and the luncheon. These strong leaders exhibited vibrant prayer lives and took every need to the source of wisdom. Every decision was bathed in prayer, everything from the gifts to give to the empowerment of the speaker's testimony with the love of God. Prayer fashioned the success of their ministry.

The sterling quality of these faithful servants of God was their adherence to the great commandment. When the religious leaders asked Jesus what the greatest commandment was, He replied, "Love the Lord your God with all your heart, with all your soul, and with all your mind. This is the first and greatest commandment. And the second is like it: 'You shall love your neighbor as yourself'" (Matthew 22:37–39).

Reflecting back on those early retirement years of being involved in two major activities at the same time, I gained a clearer understanding that it was part of His plan to reach women interested in creating needlework. One of them He had in mind was Lydia. My needlecraft representative had set up an attractive display booth of handmade stitchery items at the mall. It was a great way to meet ladies who had a desire to learn the art. That is when I met Lydia, a friendly grandmother from a nearby town who was really impressed with what she saw. When I told her she could learn to create these same beauties at the free classes we offered in ladies' homes, she was eager to hear more and filled out a slip for me to contact her the following week. Her party was a great success, with a tremendous turnout and superb sales that earned an abundance of stitchery gifts. Since she continued to book parties, as did her guests, my notebook was filled with names from her small town. Lydia was very appreciative and enjoyed helping me pick up and pack up after the parties. One day, when we were loading my truck, she spotted an open box of CWC invitations I needed to distribute.

Her many questions prompted me to ask her to be my guest. At the luncheon, she heard about a new FBC (Friendship Bible Coffee) that I would be hosting. Thinking she needed Bible knowledge to attend, she was hesitant, but I assured her all of us were beginners. The warm welcome she received kept her coming to hear the powerful truth of God's love for her. Many weeks later, at the final session of the study, Lydia received God's love and committed her life to Him!

I still get chill bumps every time I think how God used a sewing needle, an attractive invitation, a warm welcome, and an open Bible to win Lydia's heart! Retired? I cannot imagine withdrawing from any action that involves any of God's perfect plans!

Chapter 9

---✂---

SHOWERS AND STORMS

S howers of God's goodness intermingled with the storms of the world's turbulent times design the ebb and flow of each person's life cycle. There will be variations in their size and in their timing, but they are a certainty. When the calendar turned the page to the twenty-first century, I became aware that the timing of little problems had picked up the pace. Some "get up and go" was missing. We found ourselves saying "What?" to more people more often, and our medical appointments exceeded our social events. Our friends told us we were normal as they welcomed us into their club of the Golden Years. Our hearts assured us that God's grace, His perfect goodness, would enable us to weather any storm, whether a minor tremble or a major tribulation.

One morning in May of 2000, we heard the big white perch at Toledo Bend calling our names. Since it was the season to mop up and fill up the freezer with fresh filets, we packed up a week's supplies and headed to our lake house we called "The Camp." This place, our little bit of "heaven on earth" for thirty-one years, was surrounded by incredible beauty and filled to overflowing with love, laughter, peace, and joy. We looked forward to each stay as a child does for Christmas morning. We were never disappointed.

On the last day, Les was outside, tackling his last chore of mowing the grass. While standing at the fence talking to my neighbor, I noticed he was struggling. There were too many oaks and pines to circle on, too much land to cover, and it was hot. On impulse, I blurted out, "Les doesn't need this kind of work anymore. We ought to sell this place!" Little did I realize my rash remark would open a new door into the nature of God. For the first time, the light of Isaiah 65:24 reflected His omniscience (complete knowledge). In essence, He declares that even before we call on Him, He has heard and answered. Within a few weeks, I had experienced that truth. He knew it was the right time for us to say goodbye to our old friend and do it together.

The entire transaction of this unplanned sale was perfect because God was the realtor. The buyer, our neighbor's cousin, was eager to own a lake home and so easy to work with by phone. After accepting our price, he sealed our verbal agreement with a large escrow check. At the end of nonstop visitors, we set a closing date to meet with him for the first time at the lawyer's office to sign and exchange documents. With business completed, it was time to take Mr. J to see his new purchase and get acquainted with its operation tips. Getting ready to drive away for the last time, we were more than surprised when he handed us a set of keys with the standing invitation to use the camp whenever we wanted; we just had to let him know! Yes, we went one time. It became our personal closing date; it was not our place anymore.

Thank You, God, for loving us and revealing Your glory. Several weeks after basking in the warmth of God's sunshine and rejoicing over His goodness in selling the camp, a need of which we were not aware, our lives were suddenly chilled by a short but icy storm. It was a gorgeous October day, and Les was headed to his favorite fall meeting of the week, the Quarterback Club luncheon at McNeese Fieldhouse. Enthusiastic coaches would discuss Saturday night's football game with their excited fans and supporters. The "old coach" really looked forward to these gatherings and left the house in high spirits in plenty of time to drive those few blocks. Since Diane and Mark were home on furlough from their ministry post in South Africa, we were set for some catching up time, revisiting our past years' joys and challenges.

It seemed as though we had just started when the sight of a police car pulling up in the driveway engulfed me in paralyzing fear. Only when the officer opened the passenger side door and assisted a stumbling, badly shaken man to his feet did I feel God's peace return. Whatever happened during the past thirty minutes did not matter. Les was alive!

From the police officer's report, given to him by a passing motorist, Les had his accident attempting to cross a boulevard. He had stopped and looked to his left. Because he did not see the speeding car behind the curve in the road, he pulled out. The driver slammed the front side and threw the car twenty feet to land on the median. If the impact that demolished the front had occurred a few feet further back, Les would have been killed instantly! Les had experienced a miracle; we had been given a glimpse of God's glory!

Every time I think of that day, I thank God for His faithfulness to His children, to protect them. His Word tells us He "rescues us from trouble" (Proverbs 11:8) and "preserves us from all evil" (Psalm 121:7). David experienced a lifetime of God's protective hand upon him and wrote of it many times. Psalm 91 is a very assuring passage of God's protection. The truth of verse eleven was very visible on the boulevard that day. "For He shall give

His angels charge over you, to keep you in all your ways" (Psalm 91:11). How great is His faithfulness!

Eleven months after Les's miracle, America was slammed by the storm of all storms on September 11, 2001. History books labeled it "9/11." The memory of that vicious assault against our great nation was deeply carved in our minds and hearts with indelible red ink. American shores had been breached by terrorists!

The scenes on the TV screen were surreal! In a state of shock and disbelief, frozen in thought, we stared as evil pilots savagely plunged their missiles into the Twin Towers in New York City! They had hit their bullseye, the material heat of our land; they had blanketed our ground with a multitude of dead bodies and massive piles of debris and destruction. But, they had not accomplished their sinister goal to obliterate the American way of life, to destroy its values and principles upon which it had been established under God's direction. They failed because they had lost sight of our most powerful weapon, the spirit of every true American. They had nothing in their armory to defeat resilient, courageous, uncrushable people who stood tall and defiant in the battle for freedom.

Whenever I become impatient for God to execute His justice and evil, I'm reminded of the Christian victory song, Psalm 37. God tells me, "Do not fret over evildoers... for they shall soon be cut down like the grass, and wither as the green herb" (Psalm 37:1–2) and "for yet a little while and the wicked shall be no more" (Psalm 37:10)! Knowing that God is faithful to His powerful promise, I buried that "9/11" memory at the bottom of my chest.

It's time to refocus, to revisit a unique place and its people, a bountiful source of joy and laughter for many years, especially during our golden retirement season. The place: a large round table with chairs next to the prescription counter at the rear of the neighborhood drug and gift store. The people: a dozen retired men with congenial personalities from all professions with various hobbies and levels of education and faith.

Every morning, except Sunday, from nine to eleven, and every afternoon from three to five, some or all of that group would gather around the table for coffee and conversation. Frequently, the druggist (owner) would chime in while filling prescriptions. He enjoyed their company and was pleased to have a fresh brew ready when they strolled in. Their routine never changed; they picked up their personal cup from the nearby hutch, filled it half full, and headed to "their" chair. The topics for discussion never ended; they ranged from seemingly small and insignificant to weighty and burdensome. If the solutions offered for a problem became too highly opinionated, heavy bursts of laughter were sure to follow.

Club membership was exclusive, with one exception. The wives were invited to bring their cups for the hutch and join them for the afternoon sessions. The men enjoyed the feminine touch, especially when they initiated birthday celebrations. The honoree was treated with a huge cookie cake from the mall while the others stacked the table with little gifts from the handy gift section in the store. Over the years, their camaraderie forged a strong bond of friendships, genuine and tight-knit. It was well known as the "Coffee Club."

Even when the drugstore closed, the Coffee Club continued due to the generosity of Ms. B and her husband. They had an empty but furnished house two doors from their home. It was a place that needed people to give it life, and Ms. B knew the very group, the Coffee Club. Her giving heart kept on; she bought the round table and hutch as a reminder of the club's beginning. In their new location, the men got organized as to who would do what and collected dues to buy a coffee maker and coffee. After Ms. B and her husband were made lifetime members, the coffee house was officially open for business.

There is no way to adequately describe three decades of priceless memories of dearly loved people drinking coffee around that table. When I remember all the joys and sorrows we shared, the jokes and the tall tales we heard, the silly and serious gifts we gave, the snacks and meals we ate, and even the bedrooms we used for our overflow of company, I am deeply humbled by the great goodness of God. "Every good gift and every perfect gift is from above, and comes down from the Father of lights" (James 1:17). That unique place and those precious people were a gift of God's love to all of us. Yes, indeed, "the Lord God abounds in goodness" (Exodus 34:6).

On August 29, 2005, all those delightful memories of happy years with the Coffee Club suddenly scurried back into their golden treasure chest; Hurricane Katrina had ripped open New Orleans with her convulsive winds. Two days before her assault, in the caravan of vehicles headed west out of the city were our son Bob, his wife, their daughter, son-in-law, and two-year-old grandson. Our home became their refuge for three weeks, a place of comfort in which to gather information and make some plans. They learned that one home was completely demolished, and the other had livable space on the second floor. It was their only option when they returned to begin again. God was so good; at the end of the year, He had provided each family with a home! Three days after our family drove off, the alarm for Lake Charles was sounded; the mayor had ordered an immediate mandatory evacuation. Hurricane Rita had awakened and was determined to wipe our city off the map with her monstrous assault on September 24, 2005. At first, I wondered if we could tough it out. The house had proved its strength during Hurricane Audrey; a generator to power the house was connected, gasoline to operate it had been purchased, and the freezer was well stocked. I am so thankful to God that His spirit of wisdom took charge and moved us to Cindy's place in Lafayette, out of harm's way.

At the end of week one, we were allowed to "look and leave." When we returned to Lake Charles, weaving through the city streets was scary. They were partially blocked by giant stacks of uprooted trees, tangled wires, and twisted poles. The first sight of the house was sickening, with one exception: the beautiful fall wreath on the front door was intact—every sprig in place! It was the perfect sign of the hope I needed.

The visible damage identified the culprit: spin-off tornado winds. They had snapped and propelled a large pine tree which caved in the roof over the carport, den, and living area; sliced off the chimney; demolished the entire back porch; and plunged a large oak limb through a security-barred bedroom window!

Except for the nightmarish destruction in the bedroom, the rest of the house appeared habitable until we opened the front door! The repulsive stench of a week's decay of fish and meat was overwhelming. Even so, in the allotted time, our crew of four had black bagged the garbage, drove it to the dumpster, sterilized the freezer, and left it open and filled with deodorizing tablets, solutions, and powders. In six hours of daylight, an impossible task had been accomplished!

At the end of week two, electricity returned to the city, and Les and I returned home. Even though the contractor needed eight months to complete the restoration, God showered us with His blessings. We lived in the house the entire time; all structures were strengthened with steel girders in the attic; the fireplace received a new and sturdy chimney; each room was freshly painted; and we enjoyed a beautiful porch with all new furniture. The icing on the cake? A financial windfall from the government to help hurricane victims!

Once again, the truth of Romans 8:28 had been joyfully experienced. With His perfect love, God had taken a dark and powerfully destructive storm, and with His more powerful light, He had transformed a disaster for us into rays of sunshine for our good.

For sure, I will always trust my Heavenly Father, who is "like a shelter from the wind and a refuge from the storm, like streams of water in the desert and the shadow of a great rock in a thirsty land" (Isaiah 32:2, NIV).

Chapter 10

THE SUFFICIENCY OF HIS PRESENCE

S pringtime has always been my favorite season. Winter has been put to bed for a long nap. Spring has covered him with her delicately stitched quilt, a kaleidoscope of brilliant colors and unique designs. Her exquisite display has declared to all who would gaze, "Beauty has been born."

The spring of 2007 was extra beautiful; Diane and Mark had come home for a two-week visit from the mission field in South Africa! When their three U.S.-based kids piled in, the walls shook with excitement. The pinnacle of joy was reached when Diane announced, "Mark and I are moving back to the States on October 1!" And then some special sweetness, "Mom, you'll need help with your knee surgery in July, so I'm staying an additional six weeks." Those six weeks were God's gift to Mom, Dad, and "Daddy's Sugar."

Before Diane left for the airport on August 10, she followed her goodbye routine with an endless bear hug and standing order from her bright and shining smile, "When I get back and settled, I'm coming to see you two every month or two." And off she flew.

On October 1, I was jubilant. Mark and Diane had arrived safely on American soil! There would be no more long flights back to Africa for them and no more long separations for us. With God's strength and wisdom, they had emptied their home, either shipped or sold the furnishings, handled a rush of prospective buyers, and finalized the sale the day before they left. It had been six weeks of intense pressure and continued when they landed here. After an absence of eighteen years, they had to start life over. For starters, an apartment was needed in which to live, a car in which to travel, and a bank account from which to transact business. Thankfully, they had friends with whom they could stay, dear friends who provided for all their personal needs while they got established. At the end of the first week, the demands of a quick business trip to California only heightened the pressures.

During the midnight watch on October 26, Les awakened me from a deep sleep. "June, get up. Mark's brother, John, and his wife are in the living room, something about calling Mark." When they connected with him, they handed me the phone. "Hello," but instead of words, the sounds were uncontrollable sobs, over and over and over. Then, finally, reality spoke, "Mark, is Diane gone?" And his shattered heart gasped, "Yes." That deadly sound shook my entire being.

What happened next was supernatural! It cannot be explained by words, only partially grasped through experience. I sensed a strong presence of the Lord, who took off His warm robe of comfort. Then He wrapped it around me and held me tight during these dark days, weeks, and months of sorrow. He knew when it was time for me to live again and gently relaxed His tender grip.

Time in the great Physician's presence is His prescription for healing. During that time, my faith was freshly empowered by the truth of the Old Testament passages about comfort:

"I, *even* I, *am* He who comforts you" (Isaiah 51:12); "Once I have sworn by My holiness; I will not lie to David" (Psalm 89:35); and "For I *am* the LORD, I do not change" (Malachi 3:6). These are powerful rays of sunshine. In the Lord's presence, I had experienced His comfort, and I knew He would always be my Comforter.

Just as surely as Spring had covered Winter's dead leaves with the bright blanket, so did the January birth of our first great-granddaughter bury our sorrow and tears with her contagious smile. Her bubbly personality allowed no room for any gloom.

For Les, that emotional boost was only temporary. By May, his enjoyable walks were seldom and shorter while his daily naps were frequent and longer; his favorite meals, barely touched, had been replaced by high-powered, nourishing milkshakes that kept the blender burning; but the long hours together on the back porch glider, reminiscing over sixty-five years of sweet memories, were God's gift of love.

By summer, I knew that my true love would be leaving me soon. That belief was confirmed on August 15 by the report of his last scan, "a large inoperable mass; start hospice."

During Les's final twelve days on earth, seven of which he was lucid and mobile, I witnessed his gradual and perfect transition to heaven. It was the same journey that everyone who believes in the Lord Jesus Christ as their Savior takes, peaceful and hopeful. God was so gracious. Instead of a sterile hospital room, hooked to life support machines and drugged by pain-killing pills, Les enjoyed the comfort of his own bed, familiar surroundings, and loving family. Being connected to his Heavenly Father, he rested in the peace of His presence; it was sufficient.

On August 27, when the hospice nurse told me comatose patients hear every word spoken and they wait to be released, I went back into his room to express my love, assure him of my welfare, and promised him we would be together forever, as soon as I finished God's assignments. Bob and Cindy joined us with their special expressions of love. Within two hours, Les's waiting angels carried him home.

That righteous man knew the Good Shepherd and trusted in the truth of His promise. He could say, "Yea, though I walk through the valley of the shadow of death, I will fear no evil; For You *are* with me; Your rod and Your staff, they comfort me" (Psalm 23:4).

With death:

There is no fear; the comforter is present.

There is no pain; shadows cannot hurt.

There is no duration; travel through the valley.

God is gracious to His children; His presence is their sufficiency.

"I will never leave you nor forsake you" (Hebrews 13:5).

Chapter 11

PASTURES OF REFRESHMENT

Whether I trudged through a dark, stone-cold valley with a sigh or skipped along high, sun-kissed mountain peaks with a song, my Good Shepherd has provided for all my needs. A former shepherd boy, King David, proclaimed this eternal truth, "The Lord is my shepherd; I shall not want" (Psalm 23:1). The apostle Paul, chained in a prison cell, joyfully echoed the shepherd's promise, "And my God shall supply all your need according to His riches in glory by Christ Jesus" (Philippians 4:19).

Yesterday, today, or tomorrow, my God is the same. In this season of my life, He knew my need for healing and adjusting to a newly single life. He knew, and He supplied by implementing His perfect plan. He coupled my lifelong desire with a lifelong world traveler. In July of 2009, my granddaughter Leslie and I flew to our cruise ship to tour Alaska!

The majesty of God's creation there was a vision to behold. From the railing of our ship, we gazed in wonder as massive mountains reached high to straighten their snowcapped glacier. From the wide window on our cameras, we gasped as mammoth humpback whales played jump rope with the waters. From a bench in a bird sanctuary, we stared in awe at the potential powers of a giant eagle's wings that spanned six feet. Sitka, the eagle, had been rescued and rehabilitated by her trainer to whose padded arm she was chained for our viewing. Perhaps Isaiah had this powerful creation insight when he wrote, "But those who wait on the Lord shall renew their strength; they shall mount up with wings like eagles" (Isaiah 40:31).

One day, waiting to pan for gold like the miners of the gold rush era, we headed up a very steep mountain on one of their trails to make our fortune. Instead of a climb by foot with pack mules and picks, we boarded a rickety railroad car that desperately hugged mountain walls as it chugged along squeaky tracks. Even though the long ride was more than scary and our "millions" were less than $20, the level of fun that day rang the bell!

The thrill of a once-in-a-lifetime dogsled ride in snow on top of an Alaskan glacier was the highlight of our entire adventure. Before the helicopter flew us to the dogsled camp, we layered up with heavy jackets, hoods, pull-up pants, gloves, and socks before replacing our shoes with cleated boots. After our scenic flight of looking down on a canvas no artist could paint, we landed on a special glacier, the only one that welcomed its visitors with a deafening, 300-piece, all-dog choir! With sixty-mile-per-hour winds, we could not have reached our sleds if it had not been for the ropes that were fastened to sturdy poles deeply anchored into the ground. These heavy ropes enabled us to reach the other areas as well: the unheated gourmet huts where the trainers slept and the heated mess hall.

Once seven dogs were harnessed to each of the sleds, and we were seated, belted, and blanketed, there was nothing to do until the drivers sounded their signals to start the ride. When they did, it was off to the races for eager dogs and exhilarated riders. Not even freezing temperatures or fierce winds diminish the great joy we experienced that day in God's creation as we rode through Alaska's winter wonderland. That treasured memory went into the golden chest as a pure magic adventure.

When I reflected on that God-given trip, I knew I had been cared for just like His little David described in the next two verses of Psalm 23. "He makes me to lie down in green pastures; He leads me beside the still waters. He restores my soul; he leads me in the paths of righteousness for His name's sake" (Psalm 23:2–3). My Good Shepherd was the one who had supplied my needs. The one who had given me rest, nourishment, and refreshment, He was the one who had rejuvenated my entire being. He was the one who would lead me along new and exciting paths of righteousness!

Back home with a fresh zest for living, I realized my leadership role of responsibilities on the planning team of CWC. The team, challenged by new outreach goals, moved forward with the plans to implement attractive programs. I relished the continued flow of friends in and out of my home for prayer and planning.

A year after my pure magic adventure, I received a wedding invitation for my grandson Matt and his sweet Katie to come to Florida in August. It was a little bittersweet. I was excited for them but sad to think I couldn't make the trip because the macular degeneration had worsened. Shuffling through airport terminals would have been a major issue, especially with the loss of hearing. Knowing my wishes to attend this wedding, my God handled all the details. Cindy was my escort, our flights were safe, their Christian ceremony was picture-perfect, and the reception was a celebration of pure joy. As He had promised, God had supplied all my needs.

During the years following our Florida wedding, the "love bug" found new young hearts to infect with his special connection of stardust. He zeroed in on Jen (Matt's sister) and Geoff (Katie's brother) and left them with high fevers and one on bended knee! When we received their wedding invitation, we were certain of their full recovery by October 30, 2010.

Once again, I was so thankful God knew my desire to attend Jen's wedding, to fill her mom's empty chair, even though I couldn't take Diane's place. He knew, and He provided. Cindy and I flew to Georgia for the weekend of festive activities. Everything from the rehearsal dinner party, bridesmaids' brunch, another picture-perfect wedding, and a lively reception all were saturated with fun, excitement, love, and joy. A beautiful tribute to Diane concluded the ceremony when Jen and Geoff released lighted lanterns that drifted up to heaven's gate. The entire wedding had been a manifestation of God's goodness to all of us. Actually, it was a continuation of His blessings that had already framed my life.

After I reflected back on these first few years after Les's homegoing, I marveled at the phenomenal outpouring of the Shepherd's goodness. My needs had been great, but His sufficiency to supply had been greater than I ever imagined. When He had led me to and through His green pastures, He had left so many permanent fingerprints that my life was a testimony to the truth expressed by the psalmist, "The goodness of God endures continually" (Psalm 52:11). David continued this thought when he wrote, "Surely goodness and mercy shall follow me all the days of my life" (Psalm 23:6).

Another version of this verse reads, "goodness shall pursue me" seems stronger to me; I cannot escape from His goodness!

God is amazing! This Most High and Holy One left His splendor to become a shepherd and live on the lowest level of esteem; He did that to become my Good Shepherd who provided all my needs in all my seasons. He was faithful to His Word; with satisfying refreshment in sunny green pastures, He healed a little lamb.

The Lord is my shepherd; I shall not want.
He makes me to lie down in green pastures;
He leads me beside the still waters.

He restores my soul; He leads me in the paths
of righteousness for His name's sake.

Yea, though I walk through the valley of the
shadow of death, I will fear no evil;

For You are with me;

Your rod and Your staff, they comfort me.

You prepare a table before me in the presence
of my enemies; You anoint my head with oil;
My cup runs over.

Surely goodness and mercy shall follow me all
the days of my life;
And I will dwell in the house of the Lord
forever.

Psalm 23

Peace, provision, hope, encouragement, guidance, deliverance, companionship, protection, help, healing, abundant life, and an eternal, heavenly home—*all our needs are met! Nothing is lacking!*

Chapter 12

A Glimpse of His Glory

Life was good. Dreams had become realities. The move to single status had been made. From my ninety-year-old perch, I saw good health, reviving energy, and a mind and memory that continued forward in high gear. The relationship with my Heavenly Father was sweeter and closer than ever before.

Living was rich and full, with each day offering new and exciting adventures and each night providing peaceful rest. Business and relaxation had worked out a good schedule, but it was still flexible to change. God continued His plan for my service that He began thirty years ago; I was to stay focused on the Christian Women's Club and their outreach goals. That was easy because I also believed that lost sheep could be found at Christian parties, prayer coffees, and purposeful Bible studies. I was grateful to live in my home, which was an "open house" for these activities, and I was grateful for a driver's license to go and do. I was especially thankful for God's perfect love that made it possible for me to live with His abundant joy.

The day on the calendar read June 13, 2013. For me, the day began as usual, rising before dawn showing his "good morning" smile. These early hours were treasured time of complete silence, except for the loving whispers of my Father. This portion of each day was essential to living every day. As usual, this day began in my "sweet spot," a white chair in the living room facing a large picture window. From outside, the rays from a streetlight outlined my path to the kitchen, where the coffee maker was ready to deliver a cup of its fresh brew.

Within an hour in my sweet spot, what had begun as a usual morning turned dramatically unusual. A confusing thought from nowhere disrupted the silence: "Go to the DMV today and get your driver's license renewed." I was certain this was not from God. He would not say something like that. I shook it from my mind. But, in thirty minutes, when the same exact order was repeated, I used logic to deny God's involvement. He knew my birthday was three weeks away, the renewal deadline, so He knew it was not imperative today!

I thought I had dismissed this confusing order until I turned on the lamp to read the daily devotion entitled "Obedience and Reward." By the time I had read through the last verse at the end of the article, I was convicted; I knew God had spoken to me! "For the eyes of the Lord run to and fro throughout the whole earth, to show Himself strong on behalf of those whose heart is loyal to Him" (2 Chronicles 16:9).

By 10:00 a.m., I was waiting in line with my number at the DMV. When my turn came, the agent began with a few preliminary questions before she asked me to look into the viewing machine and read what I saw. It was a simple request that became an impossible task. How could anyone give meaning to dozens of scattered dashes and crazy curves? Repeatedly, I rubbed my eyes, squinted, and blinked, but nothing helped. Not knowing what else to do, I asked her if she could adjust her machine. That lady had the longest fingers and pointed one of them at me. "If you can't read that, I cannot renew your license! Try again."

When I failed a second time, I did what I should have done at the beginning of the session. I prayed. I don't remember the exact words, but I know my thoughts. "Lord, I am helpless and need You. I cannot read that screen. If I cannot read it, I cannot get my license renewed. If that is Your will, then so be it, but if You want me to have a license, then You will have to do something. I can't."

It seemed like forever that I stared at that screen, waiting for God to change it, but He never touched it. He performed an even greater miracle; He touched me! The creator of this world, God Almighty, showed me His presence. He opened my mouth, and He spoke for me! My ears did not comprehend, but the agent did, "Very good! That will be $12.50." This supernatural "glimpse of His glory" will endure for eternity in my heart.

I believe the Lord manifested His presence and His power to me to strengthen my faith. When I felt so helpless at the DMV, His presence confirmed the truth of His Word. In Hebrews, He said, "I will never leave you nor forsake you" (Hebrews 13:5), and to Jeremiah, He said, "'Can anyone hide himself in secret places, so I shall not see him?' says the Lord; 'Do I not fill heaven and earth?' says the Lord" (Jeremiah 23:24). God showed His omnipresence, everywhere present at the same time!

When God created the heavens and the earth and all living things from nothing by the power of His spoken Word (Genesis 1:1–3), He proved He was the omnipotent one who had complete and perfect power. El Shaddai, one of God's names, means "God Almighty" (Psalm 91:1). Jesus spoke of this power when He said, "But Jesus looked at them and said to them, 'With men this is impossible, but with God all things are possible'" (Matthew 19:26). To have witnessed the perfect power was unbelievable!

These fresh revelations of the magnitude of God drew me into a clear relationship with Him, of knowing Him better through more intense Bible study and more meaningful prayer time. And the better I knew Him, the easier it became to trust Him completely with all concerns and for all needs. I believe God allowed me to have a "glimpse of His glory" for a deeper relationship with Him. When God became involved in human affairs, it was the miracle He used to strengthen my faith with holy steel.

Chapter 13

Always Trustworthy

During the years following the miracle at the DMV, I spent quality time in God's classroom studying His Word. Sometimes, it was in preparation to teach CWC studies and sometimes for personal growth. When reading Psalm 139, I was impressed with God's rich description of the magnitude of God's nature. Not only was He always present (omnipresent) and had complete power (omnipotent), but God had all knowledge (omniscient). He knows when we sit down, get up, the path we will take, all our thoughts, all our ways, and all the words our tongues will speak (Psalm 139:1–4). And before we were born, He knew our future, "Your eyes saw my substance, being yet unformed and in your book they all were written, the days fashioned for me, when as yet there were none of them" (Psalm 139:16). Certainly, we can sing with the hymnist, "How Great Thou Art"! and knowing the Lord does not change (Malachi 3:6). I confidently obey His Word "Trust in the Lord with all your heart, and lean not on your own understanding; in all your ways acknowledge Him, and He shall direct your paths" (Proverbs 3:5–6).

In July 2014, I was given a new opportunity to trust the Lord; macular degeneration in my left eye was getting worse. Monthly injections offered some hope of slowing its progression, but I had no encouragement that it would not affect the other eye. Naturally, my mind shifted to the future and the impact of the disease, especially when my independence would need to yield its control. I wasn't anxious because I knew the Lord already had His good plan for me (Jeremiah 29: 11), and through prayer, He would prepare me for each step of the way in His time.

Instead of dismissing nagging thoughts and just waiting for God to develop His plan, I let logical reasoning rule. Since God will probably move me close to Cindy and Lafayette, it would be a good idea to just look at Lafayette's assisted living (AL). Because the Bible says, "For as he thinks in his heart, so *is* he" (Proverbs 23:7), you already know that I went AL shopping before His time. Cindy did some research, picked a "good" AL, arranged our visit, and off we went. On our arrival, we heard a peppy sales talk, we saw the traditional touring highlights, and we enjoyed a tasty lunch. My looking led to signing a waiting list for prospective residents, and that led to a feeling of satisfaction; the plan of where I would spend my future had been settled.

A month later, on September 30, I received a phone call from a longtime family friend. After some small talk, he told me of his friend who was looking for a house, and he had given him my address. The man liked what he saw, and my friend could bring him over. I was astonished! No one but family knew my concerns, and no thoughts of selling the house someday were voiced outside the family circle. But after a week of meetings with this couple, I knew I had a realtor, and he had initiated step one of the sale of my house!

Every aspect of God's plan was transacted smoothly around the kitchen table without lawyers to advise or official documents to sign. We were three Christians working together, making decisions for each party's benefit. Because we both needed some time for personal business, we agreed to close in March and move at the end of April. I was thankfully amazed with the way my trustworthy God worked all the details of this sale together with blessings for each of us!

After a blessed Christmas celebration at home with all my family and after the last car left, following a large U-Haul, I was a tired mix of many emotions. The rip-roaring joyful sounds of happy hearts were strangely silent, and that made me sad. Half of the house had been emptied of its furnishings, which had been loaded onto the truck and were headed to new homes; that made me glad! I was greatly relieved to see everything earmarked for Goodwill out on the back porch ready for pickup; to know the items to transport with me were boxed, labeled, and stacked in a now vacant room; and to open cabinets and closets and see nothing or only some essentials. What really surprised me was my new excitement about moving!

It was time to phone the AL to make the call I promised when I was about ready to move in. The warm and welcome words I expected had turned chilly and calculating. Somehow, my number on the waiting list was lower than I knew it should be. And somehow, they did not see any apartments becoming available for at least six months. Naturally, they were "sorry for the misunderstanding." I removed my name from that list. Because Jesus said, "Without me you can do nothing" (John 15:5), I knew I had failed because I had acted independently of Him in seeking His will.

God initiated His perfect plan when a neighbor learned of my dilemma and offered a suggestion. "Just move into the AL here in the neighborhood for the time being. You've been doing Bible studies there for years, you know everybody, and you would still be in Lake Charles." Her words made good sense! When I remembered she was a board member there, I was encouraged that this was God's direction. Within one hour, I knew that He was in control. She made one phone call; we made one visit, and one apartment was empty (just vacated)! It would be freshly painted, recarpeted, and ready by the end of April! All I could say was, "Thank you, Father God, for being so good to me."

During the few months before moving day, God's great goodness hit the bullseye; He revealed my new Lafayette permanent home, showcasing it on Cindy's computer! When she drove to the site to see, she saw a mass of wooden stakes stuck in an expanse of muddy ground. When she called the Lafayette number, it rang in another state, but the voice that answered proved to be the sweetest voice on this side of heaven. She said she would drive to Lafayette at our convenience and meet us at the place of our choosing. After our two-hour meeting with Ms. J on the veranda of a local coffee house on that lovely spring day, my heart was in full bloom!

That Christian lady expressed a true love for the elderly and their total welfare. She was excited about the services and amenities their new facility would be offering to encompass all needs for the wellness of body, soul, and spirit. The end of the visit was the end of my search for God's will. With perfect peace, I "toured" the blueprint, picked up my apartment, paid the move-in fee, and left with complete joy. Once again, He had shown me He was trustworthy.

From the Bible, I knew in my mind that I could trust Him; He was the only one who had complete power, complete knowledge, and was everywhere present at all times. Because He said in His Word, "For I *am* the LORD, I do not change" (Malachi 3:6), I knew there would never be a single circumstance with which I could not trust Him! To know these truths that God is always trustworthy is one thing; to experience their reality, which leads to a higher level of abundant joy, is a richer blessing.

Chapter 14

SOMETHING DIFFERENT

For the greater part of my life, I have enjoyed the changes I have made and most of the ones that have come my way. For me, there is an element of excitement in something different; variety is the spice of my life!

In my home, sometimes the change would be subtle or simple, like a new color on the walls or accessories in a room. Sometimes, the difference would appear more dramatically with a rearrangement of the furniture. When that thought was verbalized, Les often left wondering if his exit path to the door would be rerouted when he returned. Occasionally, I opted for a major renovation, such as building a large screened-in back porch, updating the kitchen and breakfast room area, or building a new den with a cozy fireplace. Each home improvement was an exciting blessing of beauty and comfort that raised our "Happy Home" flag even higher.

This desire of mine to create something different proved beneficial. The application of new innovations in the classroom piqued the children's interest in learning and raised their academic levels. The provision of new, interesting, and unusual information in adult Bible studies nurtured the women to seek a deeper relationship with the awesome God of the Bible. In my personal life, the desire to refashion the status quo helped to refashion me. I became flexible to the changes that came my way to easily adapt to the new and different.

April 28, 2015, was moving day, the beginning of change. The familiar would make way for things that would be different. It would be my last morning to wake up in the room where I'd slept for fifty-eight years, to sip my coffee on the old, comfortable back porch glider, and to lock the sturdy front door of a silent and empty house. The last look at the house as we drove away did not make me sad; my happy heart had carried out the most important item, my golden chest of treasured memories.

Driving up to The Manor, I was reminded at first glance of an old plantation with its white rockers waiting for a little movement and a lot of laughter. Inside the wide entrance, a semi-Victorian lobby greets each guest with a warm welcome. Seating is conveniently arranged for a group discussion or a more personal one-on-one opportunity to get acquainted. Leaving the lobby, one may enter a spacious dining area or move along a hallway to either three-story wing located on the sides of the main building. Each wing contains about thirty apartments ranging from small studies to large two-bedrooms. The rest of the well-arranged main building included a kitchen, salon, large multipurpose room, restrooms, and offices.

At the end of that long day, I was too tired to be excited but not too weary to thank God for His blessings. The truckers had been careful and completed the move without a glitch; my first-floor apartment with an outside entrance shortened their trips and eased their load. I found the soap and towels to take a hot shower, and my bed had been reassembled for a coveted night's rest!

The hours spent in the dining room at The Manor were some of my favorites, meeting old friends and making new ones. The lunchtime salad bar was fantastic! A row of white crocs set in an ice bed held an incredible variety of fresh veggies and fruit to create a super salad. I never hesitated to invite a guest to lunch and knew she would be impressed. Frequently, before dinner, one of the talented residents would sit at the grand piano near the fireplace and entertain with a few songs. The dining experience each day was delightful, especially since grocery shopping and kitchen chores were a thing of the past!

The activity director did a tremendous job keeping us motivated and moving, providing a variety of stimulating challenges and then scheduling them in the one large multipurpose room. The list included worship services, Bible studies, resident meetings, movies, demonstrations with guest speakers, games, crafts, and exercise sessions. When that list was exhausted, the bus took us to the mall, out to lunch, a drugstore, a supermarket, a bank, or a cultural performance at the Civic Center. I had to plan long to schedule a short nap!

The little lull in activities on Saturday morning motivated us to move our Bible studies to that time before lunch. The change proved beneficial; minds were relaxed, and hearts were open to hear God's whispers. And residents brought visitors! The students also enjoyed the new format of the lesson, viewing a DVD before the discussion of its principles and application. In the group were those who were satisfied to learn more about God and those who desired a new or deeper relationship with God. Yes, continual learning about God would lead to a trusting faith in God and a growing relationship with him. Frequently, those with a deeper hunger would continue their search as we sat in those front porch rockers. There was great rejoicing in heaven when they made decisions and sealed their eternal destiny.

In February, after nine months of assisted living, I was a creature of pure contentment. The blending of its exciting new adventures with my familiar routine of Christian Women's Club luncheons and meetings, church services and activities, and social events with dear friends had gone well. But one afternoon, my perfect life had an interruption. I fell, broke my left arm, and pulled it from the socket. At the end of two months of demanding therapy, I learned my driving days were over; the macular degeneration had spread to the right eye. This new limitation on my life was a big disappointment. Reflecting back seven years to the accident and disheartening medical news has given me some positive insight. As always, God was good; He protected my dominant right arm, which reduced recovery time. The physical therapist He sent was also trained to help with my vision problems. I will be eternally grateful for her advice to purchase a CCTV, a high-powered reading machine. Without it, I can neither read nor write anything! As always, God manifested His great goodness by working all things together for the good of one of His needy children (Romans 8:28).

When thinking about God's plan to relocate me to a new city, with a stopover at The Manor, I believe it was His unique introduction to assisted living, but in a familiar setting. Those months there were a sweet season of cushioning against an abrupt change and strengthening my faith walk. Then, with the August moving date set, I was eager to move to my new home at The Place, begin another exciting adventure with my Lord, and marvel at the perfect love and goodness of the awesome God of the Bible. Yes, "The goodness of God endures continually" (Psalm 52:1).

Chapter 15

---∞---

THE ULTIMATE CHALLENGE

O ut of one AL and into another, the move went smoothly. I hardly noticed the changes. There were the same warm welcomes, hugs of love, patient assistants (PA) everywhere and anywhere, housekeepers and custodians to clean and maintain, dining room delights, and rides to medical appointments.

The differences were noteworthy. The inside of the larger structure highlighted an elegant beauty in the lobbies and in several high-ceiling dining rooms. The landscaped courtyard, with its tropical décor, had replaced the row of front porch rockers. The culture of the area influenced the choice of activities offered and made the program more interesting while still meeting our needs of total welfare.

The weekly calendar listed religious services, but did not offer important Bible studies. Even though I had access to them by riding to church with another resident, I was concerned for those with limited transportation. When the thought continued, I reasoned it away for a while—it's not my responsibility. One day, my persistent concern demanded a response; God walked with me into the activity director's office to talk. I listened as she voiced some concerns and her many attempts to enlist a volunteer. Then, to my surprise, I said, "If you would like, I'd be willing to help." Her explosion of joy confirmed my belief. God had given me the responsibility of Bible studies.

I left her office, picked up my mail, and headed to my apartment with new excitement and joy. That exhilaration quickly evaporated at the sound of a faint snicker, followed by a sinister thought, "Who do you think you are? You can't see, and you can't hear, and you think you can do Bible studies?" God's answer was in the mail I held in my hand; in the first envelope was a Scripture card with the exact quote. He told me, "Even to your old age and gray hairs, I am He, I am He who will sustain you. I have made you and I will carry you; I will sustain you, and I will rescue you" (Isaiah 46:4, NIV). God is living and powerful, and I knew He would handle all the aspects of His plan!

Another resident interested in Bible study became my partner. We prayed, planned weekly lessons, and followed the same format I had used before of showing a DVD before the discussion. We took turns being responsible for and facilitating the lesson. We found a small room with a TV and began with a handful of seekers. At the end of the three years, we were excited about moving to a larger room and the blessings of the Holy Spirit; believers had grown in their faith and many unbelievers had received Jesus as their Lord and Savior. Seeing the light of God's love shine on brightly had ushered in another season of rejoicing.

Then came 2020, the year of lockdown. Residents were kept in, and family, visitors, and nonessential workers were locked out. COVID-19, the universal enemy from an eerie darkness, had aimed its missiles of fear, panic, and confusion straight at the core of all mankind. Here, in the name of safety, rules and regulations had been set, such as mask-wearing, and all group activities had been disbanded, putting Bible studies on hold. Because the dining room was closed, meals were served to the residents in their apartments. This strict quarantine drastically altered the activity program. Each phase had to be adapted for the individual to do alone in their room. One option that piqued my interest was the journaling of memories. We could choose their subject or one of our own that stimulated a happy memory, reflect upon it, and then write our story. I was amazed at how quickly the good thoughts became bright rays of sunshine that dispelled all the darkness in any day. At the end of that year of journaling, a new thought came to mind. Should I bundle those treasured memories in a binder and make copies for the kids and grandkids? It is only a thought but with one change: a book instead of a binder. It was just a thought.

By 2021, some of the tight quarantine restrictions had been lifted and group activities resumed as long as chairs were spaced several feet apart. Because my Bible study partner had moved and the larger room we needed had no TV, we switched to monthly meetings. I needed more preparation time before teaching without a DVD or notes. Thankfully, the Lord was with us and faithful to keep moving us forward in our spiritual journey. A few months after resuming Bible studies, that old idea returned of how to handle the collection of reflections written during COVID-19's dark days. My original plan had been to compile them in a small book and make copies for my kids and grandkids. But now, the thoughts were different. The faint whisper suggested some specific modifications. Instead of limiting the reflections to those already written, expand the writings that would cover a lifetime, relate them to the truth of God's written Word, and compile both collections in a book that would be available for readers beyond the family! This plan was an unparalleled challenge! Human reasoning was adamant,

"It's impossible at age ninety-eight!" But God said, "With Me all things are possible" (Matthew 19:26). By Christmas, after a season of prayer, I knew that this ultimate challenge was from El-Shaddai, His new purpose for me; that continuing with focus and diligence was imperative; and that I could trust God to be faithful to His promise. Just before Jesus ascended to His Father in heaven, He gathered His disciples together for His final words of instruction. With the authority over heaven and earth given to Him by His Father, He commanded them to preach, baptize, and teach others to become disciples. For over three years, the men had lived with Jesus, the light of the world. They had been His students learning all things about His Kingdom. It was time for Jesus to give them His new commandment, His Great Commission. They were to go to all nations and make disciples, baptizing them in the names of the Father, the Son, and the Holy Spirit. Then, they were to teach them to obey all the commands Jesus had taught them (Matthew 28:19–20). It was time for them to leave His classroom with their unique God-given gifts and make more disciples.

Today, the same marching order has been given to all who profess Christ Jesus is Lord. It is a commission that offers a multitude of spiritually rich rewards to those who accept His challenge.

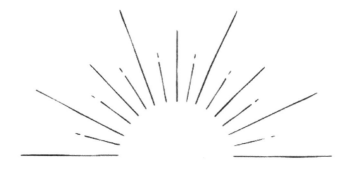

RAYS OF JOY

FOR THE DARKNESS OF

COVID-19

Chapter 16

2020

Frequently, the words happiness and joy are used as synonyms to express a feeling of elation. In reality, the source of elation for each one is different. Happiness is derived from circumstances over which there is little or no control and that are constantly changing; joy is a consistent, permanent emotion given to Christians by their indwelling Holy Spirit. It is referred to as a "fruit" listed in Galatians 5:22–23. "But the fruit of the Spirit is love, joy, peace, longsuffering, kindness, goodness, faithfulness, gentleness, self-control. Against such there is no law." Even though a Christian does not display happiness during unpleasant circumstances, the inner joy of the Lord remains strong and steady. Knowing God and trusting Him through a personal relationship with Him never changes the level of his joy.

In March 2020, the universal pandemic of COVID-19 gave birth to a season of massive destruction. Happiness, as humanity had known, received a mortal blow that questioned survival. When COVID-19 breached American shores with its missiles of terror and confusion, some people panicked and hid in their closets of isolation behind their quarantined walls. Others sheepishly braved the darkness while peering for dangers over white face masks and clutching sanitizers in both hands. For those who had experienced, "The joy of the Lord is your strength" (Nehemiah 8:10), they continued to maintain their focus on Him. In their unchanged routines, they were faithful to fervent prayers, deeper Bible studies, and long meditations. They faced each day with an attitude of calmness and strength, knowing their Father would guard them with His perfect wisdom. Thousands of years before, Isaiah promised this perfect peace when he said, "You will keep him in perfect peace, whose mind is stayed on You, because he trusts in You" (Isaiah 26:3).

And that is what I did during the scary season of darkness. His peace and direction were in proportion to my focus. The more time I spent staying fixed on serious study of His Word and in fervent prayers with Him in the stillness of the day's early hours, the brighter His light would shine for a peaceful journey.

He helped me discover extra rays of sunshine for reflecting back on His former joys. Running through my golden chest of treasured memories became a delightful experience to disperse any dark clouds. By revisiting people, places, and events of an earlier day, I was reminded of the greatness of God. Sometimes, I saw His wisdom reflected in a person; sometimes, it was His provision for visiting a special place, and sometimes it was His sovereignty in a humorous event. Because each reflection lifted my spirits, I chose a few for you and hope you will be inspired and encouraged to spend some time reflecting over all the joys of your days. Those extra rays of sunshine are a sure cure to brighten any dark day.

Chapter 17

---⋄⊱⋄---

PARENTING WITH SOLOMON

Raising healthy, God-loving children is a very challenging task in which parents need some outside help, especially from people as wise as King Solomon, who was "the wisest of all men in the world" (1 Kings 4:30–31). That advice will not be found in a book written by a single who didn't raise any children, even if the title is on the best sellers' list. Sound advice will emerge from the mouth of an experienced parent, an experience framed by sleepless rocking chair nights and 24/7 stretches of hands-on acts of love.

Especially with the firstborn, new parents begin their search among those who have a proven track record; both the parents and the child survived, and with apparent success. Guess that's why our daughter Diane called me when she and Mark were expecting their first; all of us stood strong and steady.

I remember the day she called. She and Mark were living in Florida, where he was an intern in surgery. Living four states away from home at a crucial time was scary. She asked if I would spend a week (at least) when she left the hospital. I believe "ask" is a weak word; her request was more like a calm cry of terror if I said no.

When that November day made history on their family calendar, I took the short flight from New Orleans to Jacksonville and a taxi to their apartment. Before I rang the bell, her dear door flew open to reveal a shaky new mom who had been watching from the window for security. After a warm bear hug and tears of relief, I heard, "Mom, what do we do when he starts crying?" I knew my clearly defined role and went to work. A week later, I left behind a happy trio. Mom and Dad had successfully taken their first steps in a new world of parenting a little human. Practical advice and encouraging words offered by those who have already taken this journey are beneficial, but the most reliable source of knowledge is God, who is the source of all knowledge and wisdom. This knowledge is best accessed in an atmosphere of quietness without distraction. Through meaningful conversations with God and through serious study of His Word. Only by spending quality time with the Teacher can parents be prepared to teach their children about God's amazing gift of love He has for them. Once the fundamental truth has been established in their hearts, the children will begin seeking a personal relationship with Him. Then, in the classroom of life, they will be better prepared to trudge through their valleys with strength, confident of God's presence. They will skip along sun-kissed mountain trails with joyful songs and happy hearts for God's grace. Helping their children to know God is the best gift of love godly parents can give their precious possessions. Quality time spent with God always rewards with rich blessings of "beautiful fruit." Jesus illustrated this truth when He identified Himself as the vine, and we are the branches in John 15:5. "I am the vine; you are the branches. He who abides in Me, and I in him, bears much fruit; for without Me, you can do nothing."

Quality time spent with their children is equally important in parenting. Whether it is in a one-on-one setting or in the give-and-take in group dynamics, the children must feel mom and dad's unconditional love. In this world of business, with its endless lists of "have-to's" and "want-to's," scheduling meaningful hours with children is essential. In our family, supper time was prioritized as our rock-solid bonding block. Supper time was prime time at the end of a full day to relax over a savory meal. When I sounded the signal, "Wash your hands, time for supper," our family of five hurried to their chairs. Even the Cockers quickly found their choice spots. They knew if they sat patiently and looked sad, eventually, a morsel or two would pass their way. Before a bowl was passed or a fork was lifted, Les offered a prayer to God, thanking Him for His provisions we would share and asking Him to continue caring for our family. After the blessing, the mood changed. The first give-and-take of daily events that flew from hungry mouths probably raised Emily Post's proper eyebrows. Cindy, Bobby, and Diane were full of news: the new student, a cool substitute teacher, tomorrow's school pictures, next week's field trip, a high test grade, a hard scrimmage, weekend tennis matches, or today's drill squad practice—the list was endless, but time was always available for each child to share. If a big need had to be heard, they waited until the end of the meal; a sweet dessert had to "pave the way."

I remember an "after dessert" evening when all the children presented their one big need: a backyard swimming pool. Their major reasons began with the many ways the family would save money: no more expensive family vacations, no more big gas bills due to trips to other people's pools, and no big car repair bills from extensive driving to so many entertainment places. Saving money was their trump card for having a backyard pool. Les listened patiently and intently as each child presented a part of their planned case and then suggested they research the cost of their proposal for him for their next meeting. Because the kids thought I was on their side, they chose me to do their legwork and get the numbers to ensure their needs.

That big night was one I'll never forget. Even though Les seemed oblivious to the excitement that hovered over the table, the speed in which food was devoured, or the unusually early display of sweet desserts, when the time came for him to speak, it was with the wisdom of Solomon himself. "Are all of you sure that the pool is what you want?" was followed by a very loud chorus, "Yeah!"

"You would rather have a pool than any fun-filled family vacation?"

And again, they screamed, "Yes!"

"Are you positive you want the pool instead of the ski boat?"

"*What?!*" they yelled.

"You choose, be confined to the backyard at the pool or be out on the lake in a ski boat. It doesn't matter to me."

There were two winners at the supper table that night, the boat and Les, who never wanted a boat in the first place. He won his way with wisdom and with such ease. I really believe my partner in parenting helped Solomon pen Proverbs 24:5. "A wise man has great power."

Chapter 18

THE PROMISE KEEPER

Whenever a dismal day threatens to burden your heart, bury your smile, or steal your joy, chase it away by standing strong and steady on the base of God's truth in one of His powerful promises. Our Promise Keeper has "not failed one word of all His good promises" (1 Kings 8:56).

One of my favorite promises is Romans 8:28, which reads, "And we know that all things work together for good to those who love God, to those who are the called according to His purpose." To strengthen that truth, I often reflect on or reread the related story of Joseph in Genesis 37–45. In his life, one clearly sees that God wove together all the trials and troubles of Jacob's favorite son to give birth to His new nation.

Joseph, a young Hebrew visionary, frequently boasted to his brothers about his dreams, in which they bowed down to him. His constant bragging led to their selling of him into Egyptian slavery. Joseph's life with his owner went well until his wife falsely accused him of seduction, which landed him in prison. While there, Joseph's ability to interpret the dreams of the other prisoners paved the way for his move to the palace; Pharaoh needed his dream explained. Interpreting dreams was Joseph's God-given blessing that ushered him into the role of second-in-command in Egypt, the most powerful nation in the known world at that time. His prophetic dream of a coming seven-year famine, preceded by a seven-year season of plenty, gave rise to Joseph's plan to gather and store grain for the hard times ahead, a plan that provided an abundant food supply to save all of Joseph's family. Jacob, his twelve sons, and all their wives and children were the foundation of God's fledgling nation.

Even though Joseph's story is 4,000 years old, I believe the words Joseph spoke to his brothers that day in the palace, when they realized who he was, foreshadowed the same truth Paul penned 2,000 years later to the believers in Romans 8:28. In Genesis 37–45, Joseph told his brothers not to grieve about selling him into slavery when he was a teenager; God had sent him ahead to "preserve a posterity for them on earth and save their lives" (Genesis 45:7). God had worked all things together for their good!

February 27, 1969, was a dark day wrapped in mixed emotions as Les and I laid my precious mother-in-law to rest in that country cemetery in Mississippi. Our deep sadness, knowing we would never again feel the touch of one whose heart of love was too bright for her little body, did not steal our joy of having lived with one of God's special angels. It had been twenty-five years since I first met Grandma De, as I soon called her. Six months after our wedding, Les and I took the train to Jackson, Mississippi, where Uncle John met us for the two-hour ride to "meet the family." If my nervous knees had only known this man's reputation for teasing, they would have enjoyed the ride. Once there and the introductions were finished, I knew I had worried in vain; "L.C's bride" received a warm welcome. Years later, Uncle John and I laughed about that ride when I heard his description of Grandma De, "a true Southerner who never could trust a Yankee!"

In those twenty-five years, after we moved to the South in August 1945, I was truly blessed to live near Grandma De and to see her often. What I saw was a deeply committed Christian lady who served her Lord and Savior the best way she knew— by staying in His Word. In return, her Promise Keeper filled her to overflowing levels of His amazing love, the joy of His presence, and perfect peace from trusting Him completely. She faced each day's challenges with competence, contentment, and calmness from her inner strength. In the quietness of any day, you could hear her cheerful heart hum an old gospel hymn, with her chirping canaries as a backup. Sometimes, she sang solo when her feet peddled the white sewing machine to make a new outfit for one of the children. The daily fare on the dinner table was a reflection of her diligence to coax the garden to share its bounty. Another example of her industrious nature was the maple bedroom furniture; she paid for it by getting pecans from her yard and selling them to the country store in town. She was an overcomer too. I learned that from the stories of her younger days that she told. As a teenager, she dropped out of school when her mother died to help raise a handful of siblings but went back later, finished school, and taught before she married. With her many health issues, it seemed impossible that she would have a family, her heart's desire. But "God, with whom nothing is impossible" (Matthew 19:26) blessed her with a son. Even though Les was very premature and slept in a shoe box for many months, he did survive—on sweetened condensed milk!

With God as her sufficiency, Grandma De lived the abundant life promised in John 10:10, a life that still echoes encouragement and goodness today. Little did we know that day at the cemetery that God, for another season in our lives, would continue to richly lavish us through the death of His daughter.

Since Les was an only child, he inherited all the rental properties and Grandma De's furnished home. After a few treasured remembrances had been selected by the family, a big question arose: "What do we do with all her old comfortable furniture?"

"That's simple," said my friend, "just build a second home at Toledo Bend Lake where you and Les enjoy fishing and put everything there."

Not so simple, only more questions: "Who would build it? Where to find a lot? Who would finance the loan? How could we afford the payments?" Our Promise Keeper knew each answer and led us to a waterfront lot in beautiful Pirates Cove, a patient contractor who did a super turnkey job, and to the right banker, who was our personal friend, Mr. Charley. In those days, transactions were informal. All that was needed was some sheet of paper on which the banker wrote the date, the amount of the loan, and a maturity date. After both parties signed, the deal was sealed with a firm handshake and a few words of "small talk." And, yes, God worked out the payments to the bank, too. The income from the rental properties was used to pay off the loan in six years!

Les and I were still working when we moved Grandma De's furnishings in August 1999, so going to the "camp" on weekends was a perfect blend of everything good. With great excitement, we anticipated finding the honey holes of big fish calling our name; we relished the beauty and quietness of pressureless hours away from work; and we basked in the luxury of sipping our morning brew on the front porch, sitting in those familiar white rockers as we greeted day's first smile. When it was Les's afternoon nap time on Grandpa's seven-foot wide couch, I would remember that sweetheart with sparkling blue eyes overshadowed by his snow-topped thick hair. Because of health issues, he was retired from various occupations; he managed a pure oil station, operated a dairy business, a recreational facility, and built houses to rent. Now retired, his daily schedule included a quiet nap after lunch on his long couch. When our family visited, Les and I liked that idea, but not our three little humans for whom it was a huge challenge. On one particular visit, nap time began well for the first ten minutes. Then Grandma De witnessed their one and only failure. Bobby came out of his room for the third time with the same question, "Is it time to get up?" he said. Grandpa slowly raised up, gently lifted the white napkin off his eyes, quickly pointed his index finger at the boy, and with a strong, deep whisper, "Boy, back in that bed; do not show your face until I call your name!" That was the first and last of failed challenges! When Les and I retired from our jobs, we had the luxury of retiring from the "weekend warrior gang" of fishermen and joining the "home folks" group. The quieter, less crowded weekday waters were more conducive to serious fishermen. Making these switches left the camp available for others to enjoy our blessings.

One group that accepted our invitation was Chi Omega sorority, to which our daughters belonged. It did not take long for the Owls to stake their claim and name it "Hooters Haven." Their hand-painted sign of a bikini-clad owl holding her fishing pole was a visible welcome that hung on a tall pine near the gate. Especially during the weeks of preparation for rush week, the camp was packed with wall-to-wall bodies that never slept and giggling mouths that never closed. Even today, if you listen carefully, you will hear a group of wise old Owls telling a choice tale of an earlier day at "Hooters Haven."

Divorce is a devastating situation of separation for both the child and the missing parent. The child wonders why Daddy isn't around to drive him to school, read his favorite bedtime story, or sit in his empty chair at dinner. Dad's thoughts are continuously interrupted by his own set of wondering questions.

When our son and his four-year-old son had to live with this pain, God already had His perfect plan of comfort and peace; the camp would become their fertile oasis for building healthy relationships and healing broken hearts. Whether it was during the earlier years of weekend visitations or when our grandson drove down with his dog, the camp was a taste of heaven on earth. With Grandpa as the fishing guide and me as the chief cook, their rays of joy shone even brighter. Those early years of little boy Easter egg hunts, sled skiing, and bedtime stories seem to mesh so quickly into "landing the big one" to filet and fry, flying tall over the waters behind the boat, and spending quality time in sharing their lives.

For two decades, God had provided His choice of place to mend some broken vessels. By being saturated with a genuine love of family, the camp was the right place. With abundance, God had filled it to overflowing with hours of healthy and happy activities that guaranteed His restoration. And through it all, He, once again, demonstrated the truth of Romans 8:28: He was the Promise Keeper. He had taken all the ugly scars of separation, and as only God can do, He transformed them into a lasting relationship between healed hearts.

To be able to have confidence in a promise-keeping God whose Word is true (John 17:17), who cannot lie (Titus 1:2), and who cannot change (Malachi 3:6), is a very bright ray of joy!

Chapter 19

---∞---

QUESTIONS NEED HONEST ANSWERS

When God created children, I believe He gave them an extra set of the curiosity gene; they never seem to run out of questions that need answers. The credibility of this observation was confirmed from my years in the classroom, especially in summer programs working with gifted children.

Recently, when some great-grandsons visited, one of them popped out with, "GiGi, are you as old as Martin Luther King?" To which I replied, "Yes, even older." That answer triggered an instant, deafening "Wow" and an e-mail list that next week. He and his brothers had important questions about my life as a child in the "older days." Reflecting back to that bygone era when time traveled slower, to enjoy the pleasure of life was truly a joy-filled adventure. I chose these to share:

#1: "GiGi, did you have chores?"

"The bedrooms in our house were upstairs, so there was always something that needed to go up or something that needed to be brought down, always. That something was called the "bundle," and it was my responsibility to move the bundle to its proper place. If I made a trip without my companion, I did not enjoy my restrictions! The other chore was Saturday morning dusting of the four bedrooms and the staircase railing, all before any play time."

#2: "Did you get an allowance?"

"Are you kidding? No parent paid their kids for doing what was expected of them if they were a member of the family. But whenever I did something "extra," later I would find a small "reward" on my dresser, which I saved to spend another day. An example of an "extra" was making lunch on

Monday. After Mom had spent all morning in the basement doing the weekly washing, she really appreciated coming up to eat her favorite pancakes. In those days, kids in elementary school ran home for an hour lunch break because there were no cafeterias. In the long run, I was the winner with no allowance. If I "needed" something, I would ask for the money to buy it. If I planned my speech well, I lucked out, usually."

#3: "What was your favorite book?"

"A Nancy Drew mystery. They were so exciting, the kind you read in bed with a flashlight! There were dozens of them, and I wanted all of them. The problem? They only came hardback, were very costly, and were not available on library shelves, but I had every one! Now you know why not getting an allowance was a better deal."

#4: "What was your favorite game?"

"No game was, or still is, as great as Monopoly. Ours stayed out on the dining room table for immediate use at any given time. The only exception was when company came to eat. When the cousins wanted to play, the front porch card table served as the new host."

#5: "What did your family do for fun?"

"For the most part, our pleasures were simple: going to the movies twice a week, big family picnics with all my cousins and their parents on July 4th and Labor Day, a game of croquet in the backyard, ice skating at the school's rink, cheering me on in a school play, or eating out for a very special occasion. The great event of the year was the summer vacation trip to a plush fishing resort, sometimes up into Canada. This adventure would include a visit to an educational site like an exciting Native American reservation with its "smoking" teepees and craft demonstrations."

#6: "Did you have a pet?"

"Sadly, no. Living in the North with a lot of freezing cold weather was not a good place to raise a dog, especially without a fence. Since there was no way to convince my mom to have one inside, I had to wait until I became "Mom," and then our family loved eight special pets: Tiny. Missy, Inky, Fella, Flicker, Lancer, Belle, and Schatz. I surely hope God has a yard for them in my heavenly home."

#7: "What was your biggest mistake?"

"Thinking about all my big mistakes made me realize that all of them were the result of one big mistake. I had waited too many years, until age twenty-eight, to ask Jesus to forgive me of all my sins and come into my life to be my Savior and Lord. Before I asked Jesus, I knew a lot *about* Him from my parents and going to church, but I did not know Him personally. Ever since I received Jesus into my heart as my best friend, I have experienced His great goodness and His amazing love."

Those little boys knew I loved them, so it was natural for them to ask me their important questions. To believe I had their answers and to trust me to give them honest answers. Their childlike faith in me will be necessary one day to believe in and trust Jesus (Matthew 18:3).

On that special day, they will receive a special name from their loving Father. "As many as received Him, to them He gave the right to become children of God, to those who believe in

His name" (John 1:12) and "Behold what manner of love the Father has bestowed on us, that we should be called children of God!" (1 John 3:1)

On that special day, they will receive their Father's phone number: Jeremiah 33:3, "Call to Me, and I will answer you, and show you great and [a]mighty things, which you do not know." In these sweet prayer conversations with their Father, they will never need any electronic devices, never get a busy signal, recorded messages, or voicemail, and never check the hour before dialing; they will always hear His voice, giving them honest answers to all their important questions.

Chapter 20

---∞---

CONTROLLED FREEDOM

March 13, 1999, was a red-letter day on our calendar; a baby had been born. He was the cutest bundle of joy. In six weeks, we had to adopt him! The vet told us he and his two brothers were doing fine with their mom and new teddy bear toys. On my first visit, at first glance, these miniature schnauzer puppies looked alike, all black. On closer inspection, I spotted a tiny white dot on one of their necks, the one that already had caught my attention. I liked his spunky spirit and independent nature. This little fella did not need any help getting to the chow line or sniffing out his own teddy bear to cuddle. After a few more visits, I knew he would be Les's birthday present in May.

A year earlier, this gift would not have been a wise idea. Les was still in some frame of mind as when he had to put down his two labs that were suffering from intense joint pain, "No more dogs." But my desire to have a house dog returned, and so did fervent prayers to God to help. In a few months, I decided to test the water to see if God had heard me. "Honey, do you know what I'd name a new dog? I'd call him Schatz." When Les said, "Why would you pick that name?" instead of "June, get that idea out of your head," I knew God had softened his attitude. My search began. Schatz never knew that the only way he made it through our door was because he was a "holy dog."

It did not take long for the little king to enjoy his kingdom. He had protection: a fence circled his palace. He had provision: tasty food and fresh water were served regularly. He had the presence of 24/7 help: just one bark, and his faithful servants appeared. He had companionship: dozens of squirrels to entertain him daily. And he had complete comfort: large shade trees fanned cooling breezes on hot summer days while thick green grass offered warm palettes for chilly fall naps. Schatz had the freedom to chase his activities within the enclosed environment we had established for his good.

Several years later, his strong, independent spirit motivated a poor choice. It was the day the carpet cleaners had come to do an all-morning job. Because the men would need access to the water faucet inside the gate, Schatz had been confined to the back porch. After the workers finished loading their truck and drove off, it was time to turn the little fella loose. Thirty minutes later, when my backyard neighbor called with, "Is Schatz inside? I thought I just saw him racing down my street?" my heart sank! With a quick "thank you" and a quicker search of the yard, only to find an open gate, I grabbed the car keys and was out the door. Before I could shut it, the black arrow whizzed past me to the target, his water bowl. He lapped and lapped and lapped until, finally, his feverish, exhausted body flopped to the ceramic floor for cooling and rest. His entire afternoon was completely motionless. I do not know the extent of the new adventures he had or the unusual sights he saw on his great escape, but I do know they made a lasting impression upon him. No matter how often the gate was opened to roll the garbage can to the curb or the water sprinkler to the front yard, the lure of a "better life" never enticed him again. I guess he realized he really was a "holy" dog living in the "promised land"!

Schatz's story parallels the life of a child of God. Each individual has the free will to make life choices as he lives within the perimeter of God's perfect, established will. God has the right of prime power, for the Bible tells us, "The Most High is sovereign over all kingdoms on earth" (Daniel 4:25, NIV). And because sovereign God is good (Psalm 106:1), His child knows that "No good thing will He withhold from those who walk uprightly" (Psalm 84:11). And the child also knows his father's good plans will give him a future and a hope (Jeremiah 29:11).

Sovereign goodness inspires each of His children to be confident in trusting Him completely and then to experience the rich blessings of living with controlled freedom.

Chapter 21

---◦◦◦---

IT'S ALL ABOUT TRUST

Reflecting upon some of my theological beliefs, especially in whom I trust, I recognized my focus had been consistent. During childhood, parents had taken precedence. In my turbulent teens, my know-it-all self vied for the top place. As a young adult, my independent nature delegated the control to you-know-who, and with marriage and the big responsibilities of raising children, all the troops in the advice patrol were quickly recruited. But when Jesus became my Savior, He became my Lord, the One in whom I would trust. Confident He was the truth and the light, I knew He would be my sufficiency.

But as I related to an earlier chapter, after enjoying the peaceful closeness of my journey with Him, I gradually allowed the thief of business to start slipping around; before long, I was missing golden nuggets of peace. Then, one night in a church service, God touched my heart. He wanted my completely surrendered will. His Word was clear, "You (God) will keep him in perfect peace whose mind is stayed on You, because he trusts in You" (Isaiah 26:3). His promise of peace was my stepping-stone to a renewed life of focus and trust in Him.

The Teacher directed me to the fisherman's words, "Cast all your cares upon Him for He cares for you" (1 Peter 5:7). From having watched shrimpers cast their huge and heavy nets, I knew my muscle of trust would be strengthened with each cast. As I began releasing my concerns and seeing that His way and His time far exceeded my hopes, I found it easier to entrust all my burdens to Him. Whether they seemed small and significant or gigantic with impossibilities, they became His concern. To me, this anonymous acronym for "cast" sums up God's advice for His perfect peace:

*C*ommit all your cares and concerns to Him.

*A*sk Him for His help.

*S*urrender your will to His will.

*T*rust Him to handle your burden.

With past commitments, God provided opportunities for me to evaluate any progress. My renewed pledge at the church service was no exception. A few weeks later, our oldest daughter Cindy called me late at night with a surprise announcement: she was leaving her secure vocation for a new life in full-time Christian ministry. Instead of listening to her season of prayer with God before making her decision or remembering her dad's and my trust in God to lead us on our "absolutely impossible" mission, I spoke without thinking, filled her ears with too many negatives, and ended the call in complete frustration. The "old" me had really failed the first test! Before going to bed, I asked God for His forgiveness for not trusting in His will for my child. My call to her the next morning was an acknowledgment of God's perfect will, a confirmation of her decision, and a restoration of His joy for both of us.

Over the next twenty years, my list of concerns appeared endless, but progress in casting skills was steady. When we heard our youngest daughter, Diane, and her husband, Mark, had accepted a call as medical missionaries, that was great. When they added "to Africa," my heart skipped a beat—our three grandchildren would be 1,000,000 miles from us! All of those treasured trips to Baton Rouge and Atlanta for sweet hugs and kisses and for storing up incredible memories would be replaced with their too-short, whirlwind, annual furloughs to Lake Charles. When they left in the fall of 1989 for the Ivory Coast, later to South Africa, they carried a new camcorder and a fax machine. We cherished the stacks of DVDs they continued to send and the daily love notes and artwork the phone wires slipped through the fax. The world of electronics became a happy bridge over that eighteen-year separation. From their thrilling stories of God's amazing work in Africa through His many, many faithful servants, we knew that we knew that our personal cost was minimal in comparison.

As the years passed and the grandchildren became adults, each one took a turn in making the US their new home. That's when furloughs gathered the three separatists together for family reunions, first at a Florida beach and then in Lake Charles. The year 2007 was an exception. There were two extremely different visits. The second one did not include the beach.

When the entire family arrived after a week of fun in the sun, they were so silly with excitement. All talked at once, and I heard nothing until Diane said, "Mark and I will be making our first trip from Africa in October when we move back home!" I was ecstatic! Her one statement was a lifetime of Christmas blessings. The joy that ruled supreme that week overflowed when I learned Diane was going to stay an extra six weeks to help during my recovery from knee surgery in early July. That togetherness time with Les's "Sugar" was heaven on earth for us, a precious love gift from our heavenly Father. On August 10, it was time for Diane to make her final trip back to Africa. After she had given us her long bear hugs, she cautioned me not to start crying this time. She was coming back and would see me soon! At that moment, I could have walked to the moon with the strength of my joy! On October 1, after seven weeks of 24/7 nonstop business—showing and selling their home, disposing of or packing furnishings to ship, and squeezing in sad farewells with dear friends—two exhausted bodies had completed their final trip from Africa. Staying with friends in Philadelphia was a true blessing during the next three time-demanding weeks. Having lived out of the country for eighteen years, they had to open a bank account, purchase a car, and hunt for a furnished apartment to call home until their furniture arrived. In addition, they made a quick weekend flight to California for an important meeting.

It was around midnight on October 26, the darkest hour of the night, when I was shaken from my sleep and told of Diane's passing. Even in that frozen instant, when my heart stopped beating, I knew the presence of the Lord. He had taken off His warm robe of comfort and peace, wrapped it around me, and held me tight through the tempest. This darkest hour of night ended sometime before dawn, with His sheep asleep in His arms.

After the autopsy and a private time with Diane, Mark and his children flew her home to Lake Charles, her last flight in a fifty-six-year journey. In planning her funeral, the gravesite was at the top of their list. But God had already taken care of that need. Many years before, He had stopped all of my attempts to sell or give away our choice of cemetery deed; He was protecting it for this day!

Her "Celebration of Life" service was a true celebration of joy in the midst of deep sadness. The glowing testimonies of her life by family and friends, the stirring sounds of rhythms and beats of African music, and God's Words of comfort from His book of truth were rays of joy that dispelled all darkness within our hearts. We had experienced the reality of Philippians 4:7, "The peace of God, that passes all human understanding, will guard your heart and mind through Christ Jesus." This promise from our faithful Father is for all His children who "keep their minds stayed on Him because they trust in Him" (Isaiah 26:3).

When I had to travel that same cold and deep valley road ten months later with my true love, my Lord was present with His warm robe of comfort and peace, which He wrapped around me. He held me tight, never turning me loose through the storm. He never changes! It is all about trusting Him.

Chapter 22

---∞---

HURDLES, NOT OBSTACLES

The orchestration and timing of moving into the new assisted living community were perfect—it had to be God's plan. Being one of the first move-ins during the grand opening in August 2016, I had time to get settled before meeting the other new residents as they arrived. A super activity director had scheduled a wide variety of mix-and-mingle get-acquainted ice breakers. The weekend schedule provided rides to our church services, but the weekly events lacked any opportunities for spiritual growth. When I started praying about this need, God started placing the answer on my shoulders. As the burden became heavier, so did my conviction that I was to initiate Bible studies. Knowing and doing hesitated traveling together. I had more excuses to stall than a porcupine has quills.

Oh, finally, Determination Day arrived. With superhuman strength, I headed to the assisted living office with one rehearsed question, "Would you like me to do some Bible studies?" She shot up from her chair and whirled around with one explosive question, "You would do that?" She was beyond happy with my "Yes" and so eager for me to set it according to my time; she would work around me! I committed, too, and was overflowing with joy, the kind that parallels obedience to God's will. I left her office with a bounce in my step and a song of praise in my heart.

On the way to the elevator, I stopped to pick up my mail. I was startled by a sudden, inaudible voice within, a sneering sound. "Who do you think you are? You can't read, you can't hear, and you think you can teach Bible studies?" An eerie weakness engulfed me. I could not read anything unless I laid it on my CCTV reading tray; I could not hear anything except for the highly tuned hearing aid in my better ear. What have I done? The first piece of mail I opened had my answer. On a card, God wrote, "Even in your old age and gray hairs I am He, I am He and I will sustain you; I have made you and I will carry you; I will sustain you and I will rescue you" (Isaiah 46:4, NIV). It was exactly what I needed. God had confirmed I was on the right track. It was only a hurdle of doubt set up by the "deceiver"; it was not an obstacle that would impede God's will.

Whether we call him the deceiver, the dragon, or the devil, he is Satan, the adversary of God and all who claim the name of Christian. The resurrection of Jesus from the grave was his demise; he had lost the war of rebellion against God in eternity past. He still continues his attempts to halt God's work and still battles for more souls to take with him to the pit in the eternity future. I found it wise to read a brief summary of his resume in Ezekiel 28 and Isaiah 14. He is our enemy.

In the beginning of time, God created a very special angel named Lucifer, the "light bearer" or "shining one." He was perfect in beauty, adorned with many precious stones, perfect in wisdom, and perfect in all his ways. This anointed cherub of God had been gifted with great musical talents in playing heaven's instruments and led the glorious worship and praise services to the Most High God. Lucifer lived on the mountain of God—until iniquity entered his heart.

When God heard his thoughts: "I will be worshipped by the congregation as God; I will sit on the throne of God; I will become the Most High God" (Isaiah 14:1,3 paraphrased), He revealed Satan's sin of pride, "Your heart was lifted up because of your beauty; you corrupted your wisdom for the sake of your splendor" (Ezekiel 28:17). When Lucifer elevated himself higher than God, God cast Satan down from His holy mountain; he never had been cleaned from sin.

When Satan failed to rule in heaven, he began his new campaign in the perfect garden with God's perfect people. Adam and Eve had been given only one commandment from God, who spoke to Adam. "Of every tree of the garden you may freely eat; but of the tree of knowledge of good and evil you shall not eat, for in the day you eat of it you will surely die" (Genesis 2:16–17). That's when Satan showed up in the garden to have a little conversation with Eve through the mouth of the serpent, tempting her to doubt and deny God's truth and rebel against Him (Genesis 3:1–5). When Eve looked at the fruit of the forbidden tree, she saw how good it appeared, how pleasant it would taste, and therefore, how wise she would be and become just like God. Eve believed Satan's lies; she took, she gave to her husband, and they ate (Genesis 3:16, paraphrased).

Since the adversary has not changed the tactics he used in the garden at the Fall of Man, this review of his resumé was beneficial before beginning God's new assignment. I would be more alert and better prepared to handle the hurdles he had set along the track.

A partner, a plan, and a place—all blessings to launch forward in early 2017! Another resident volunteered to help plan and conduct some studies. After praying and talking, we decided to use our favorite teacher-preacher's DVD studies for each lesson, summarizing his focal points and handing out a copy of the outline with the Scriptures for meditations. We altered the leadership role for each new six or ten-week theme. Splitting responsibilities allowed each of us more preparation time.

Our small room had a large TV screen but a very unfriendly recorder for the DVD, a real time-steeler hurdle. The glitches were so frequent they added humor and wonder about what would happen next. But for three years, nothing could impede God's love as He touched hearts and changed lives through the study of the Word! When the pandemic fire deadly missiles of fear and confusion, "quarantine" became the law of the land, and group activities joined the "closed door" list. Even though meals were served in our rooms with seating for one, we did keep in touch by phone or from masked mouths as we passed in the halls getting exercise.

Many months later, when restrictions slowly lifted and some normalcy returned, we were excited to ease back into Bible study in a very large room with widely spaced chairs but no TV. Since my partner had moved out of town, I was completely dependent upon the Lord to teach His Word. I was confident He would handle this need because He promised me that "I can do all things through Christ who strengthens me" (Philippians 4:13).

For each step, the Lord was with me. He was faithful in giving me direction, such as moving to monthly meetings and allowing more quality time for prayer and planning, and He was amazing in demonstrating His power, such as enabling me to teach an hour's lesson without notes. Whatever my need, my Promise Keeper provided. Once, when I did not ask Him in prayer first before the meeting, I opened the door to the enemy to set up a hurdle of confusion. After introducing the lesson, I had a sudden lapse of memory. I stopped immediately, we prayed, and the hurdle vanished. The Lord heard, and the Lord answered immediately. From that experience, I truly learned the source of my strength!

That final year of teaching—before launching forward with writing this book—was a refreshing time of renewal. Once again, I was reminded of the sovereignty of God as it relates to His Word. God told the prophet Isaiah that the words from His mouth would never return void. They would always accomplish His purpose and do what He sent them to do (Isaiah 55:11, paraphrased). Throughout the time of sharing God's Word with the group, I had seen the truth of this Scripture manifested in changed lives—a beautiful ray of joy to see. From teaching, I learned that if I placed life's apparent obstacles in God's hands, they became challenging hurdles He used to grow my faith. He empowered me to live in the realm of complete trust in Him and in His Word—the treasured ray of joy to experience.

There are no insurmountable obstacles for a child of God; they are only challenging hurdles for the child in which His faith will grow.

Chapter 23

NOTHING WASTED

If I had rummaged around in the attic of my parents' home, I'm sure I would have found a plaque that read "Waste Not, Want Not." Nothing was thrown away! If it wasn't recycled in the house, the garage or garden inherited the item. You don't believe me? Read on.

Mom's delicious meals usually vanished at our first seating, but if not, containers of leftovers were stacked in the fridge for a tasty snack or added to tomorrow's menu. The large brown bags that toted the groceries to the kitchen soon lined the under-the-sink trash cans that took bottles and cans. Any glass jars with screw top lids found their niche in my dad's basement workshop. Whatever he needed for his projects was clearly visible. The pages of colored comics in the Sunday newspaper were fun for wrapping kids' gifts. When neatly folded, they joined the box of shiny, glittering Christmas wrappings that would be enjoyed again. Mom's darning basket always had a pair of sad socks whose holes needed her magic needle that always made them look new again. Flannel shirts too worn to wear were ripped into rags after their buttons had been rescued for the "emerging" button box. Small tins with meds from the drugstore became handy havens for safety pins, while the grocery store's larger, more decorative ones hid Mom's fancy Christmas cookies made before the holiday rush. Even though there is more proof, believe me when I say my parents wasted nothing!

It must be a heavenly trait because God does not waste either. The Bible is filled with stories of Him using anything and everything to accomplish His purposes. When His chosen people cried out from the Egyptian shackles of slavery for 400 years, He heard and sent one to deliver them to their Promised Land. Through a wooden staff in the hands of His servant Moses, the people would experience God's presence and mighty power. When Moses threw the wood down, it became a live snake, and when he picked it up, it became a staff. The first plague against the Egyptians, turning their waters into blood, occurred when Moses struck the water with his staff. The nation of Israel had begun its journey with God's presence and a wooden rod (Exodus 3–14).

When the armies of Philistria and Israel faced each other from mountains on either side of the Elah Valley, they did what armies often did to avoid excessive bloodshed. Each army would send its champion warrior for a one-on-one combat. The army of the winning warrior would be declared the winner of the battle. Who would Israel send? Who could contend against the giant Goliath? God knew. A young shepherd boy named David would go in the name of his Lord God; he would be victorious over a pagan who defied the Almighty God of Israel. With the power of God's presence and equipped with one small stone from his creations, David released his holy weapon from his sling to strike and kill a mortal giant, a spiritual enemy of his God. It was just one small stone, but it was in righteous hands (1 Samuel 17).

In the New Testament, we read of some scribes and religious Pharisees who caught a woman in adultery and brought her to Jesus. Their purpose was to test and trap Him by using the law of Moses concerning stoning the woman to death. After some dialogue, Jesus told her accusers that whoever was without sin let him be the one to cast the first stone. Then He stooped down and, with His finger, began to write on a tablet of dirt. We don't know His message, but I believe the accusers did; one by one, they left without condemning her. A dirt tablet in the Savior's hand became a platform of hope with forgiveness for a sinner (John 8:1–11).

One day, when Jesus and His disciples came upon a beggar blind from birth, the disciples asked a common question, "Whose sin caused his blindness, his or his parents?" Jesus told them neither one, but it was for the purpose of revealing the mighty, good works of God in him. Jesus used His saliva and some dirt to make a clay paste with which He anointed the blind man's eyes. All the beggar had to do was obey Jesus and wash in the pool of Ailoam. He went, he washed, and he saw! A saliva-based clay miracle! (John 9:1–6)

Whether thousands of years ago or yesterday, God does not change; He still uses both natural and unusual circumstances to fulfill His will. When I reflected on my life experiences, I found plenty of proof of that truth. Some of the real "movers and shakers" are worth sharing.

To begin this saga with my "soul mate," God moved Les from the South to Chicago for me to meet and marry (World War II and a blind date). After fifteen months of heaven-on-earth, my spiritual journey began with a very loud wake-up call (the death of our first son). To separate me from everyone and everything upon which I had depended for twenty-two years in order to rely on Him, He provided a coaching job for Les in the South (football).

Seven years and three babies after our move to an entirely different culture in Mississippi, I was convicted of my sin and received Jesus as my savior (a question from our five-year-old daughter). To prepare me for a humanly impossible challenge facing us in two years, I needed intense Scripture study to grow my baby faith (secretary to our new "on fire" pastor). It was a two-year feast at the Lord's banquet table, which ended suddenly (a phone call from an unknown college president who began the conversation with "God said..."). Whoever heard of building a complete athletic program for men at a dying college for women? God knew, and He did it in two years! An incentive for success within two years was a football stadium in the third year was only a dream (broken promise). The move to Louisiana College for one year was bittersweet, with poor pay and working conditions for Les, but a college degree in teaching for me (a third phone call from McNeese State University with an exciting career challenge for Les). The old green Chevy, with its crew of five, made its final move to Lake Charles in 1957!

Grandma DeVall continued to love us even after we said goodbye at the cemetery in 1969 (Les's inheritance built and maintained the camp). For thirty years, it was our perfect R&R, a true haven in "storming" times. When the day came for us to say a final thank you to Grandma DeVall for this love gift, our Realtor took charge (His buyer called us from out of the blue). That sweet blessing ended in an easy sale. To remove the world's mold of excessive business, God reminded me of eternal values in the least likely effective way, in my opinion (a gaudy, boisterous revival preacher). I'm sure He smiled big the night I submitted to His Lordship a launching pad for an exciting new ministry with the Christian Women's Club (a friendly stranger in the seat next to me at a McNeese basketball game). Involvement in CWC broadened through their Friendship Bible Coffees because of my love for teaching His Word. Then, with my joy in doing needlework, He opened an outreach door (direct sales in needle crafts). The ladies I met here were invited to CWC, and many realized profound life changes by attending Fellowship Bible Church.

When the calendar turned the page to the twenty-first century, the first eight years could be described as troubling times. Maybe the ominous attack against America by terrorists on 9-11, 2001, was an eerie foreshadowing. Four years later, we saw the devastating power of Hurricane Katrina on Bob's home and experienced the destructive wrath of Hurricane Rita on ours. In 2006 and 2007, I underwent two major surgeries followed by successful recoveries and increased physical strength. God knew I would not need this surplus to deal with some dark days ahead. I faced the first one on October 26, 2007, the day Diane dropped dead at age fifty-six. Little did I know then that I would travel that same stone-cold valley road on August 27, 2008, this time alone. My true love passed through those Pearly Gates to his heavenly home.

During the next four years, as God blessed me with His comfort, healing, strength, and a new zest for living, I also experienced many new changes. When filling out familiar identification forms, I found it difficult to skip "married" to check "widow"; when I was invited to an enjoyable couples' function, I hesitated longer and left earlier; when vision list numbers were recorded, they read "legally blind," and while driving my car, blasting car horns were barely audible. God knew He needed to change my circumstances. Independent living was no longer an option (His buyer appeared at my door!). That surprise was God's clear message to me, and the smooth sales transaction was His confirmation.

Over the next few months, God closed doors on my poor choices for an assisted living in Lafayette near Cindy. His place there was not finished yet! Until then, He opened a closed door for a temporary assisted living apartment in Lake Charles. It was a great introduction to that new lifestyle and still living in familiar surroundings. On the first Friday in August 2016, His place in Lafayette became my new home where His purposes for my life would continue.

Through my century of experiences, the awesome God of the Bible continued to reveal the magnitude of His attributes in a variety of ways. Each one nurtured confidence in Him; He has all power, all knowledge, and is always present everywhere at the same time; He is the God of perfection.

Some 3,000 years ago, mighty King David bowed his knee before Him and penned a powerful description of the omnipotence, omniscience, and omnipresence of our incredible Sovereign. Each reading of Psalm 139 is like receiving an infusion of spiritual steel. One of my favorite rays of joy is Psalm 139:16. "Your eyes saw my substance, being yet unformed. And in Your book they all were written, the days fashioned for me, when is yet there were none of them."

In Psalm 139, which verse will you choose to strengthen your faith in the God of perfection who wastes nothing?

Chapter 24

---◇---

THE CELEBRATION OF A CENTURY

The pinnacle of all birthday parties that ever were given or ever will be given was reached on the weekend of Saturday, July 1, and Sunday, July 2, 2023, in Lafayette, Louisiana, at my one-hundredth birthday party! I cannot begin to list the names of so many wonderful people who helped put it together; too many hide in the wings, but I will name the angel I know who started the ball rolling after my ninety-ninth birthday party a year ago: my granddaughter Leslie carried the heavy plan of success over the finish line! Thank you, Leslie, for the celebration of a century!

Before I describe the details of that fabulous party, I need to fill you in on the previous week since it sets the stage for one more story of my Lord Jesus's sovereign power of protection His children have. Because numerous health issues had plagued me during the week and AC problems popped up Friday at bedtime, it was natural I pushed the concern button—would I make the party on Saturday? Since Lafayette was in the midst of a devastating heat wave, I was naturally alarmed when the living room unit belched its final burp of chilly air before dying in silence. When I checked the bedroom unit and saw it had stopped before reaching the seventy-three-degree setting, I knew big problems had invaded my apartment! Maintenance arrived and quickly found the problem in the bedroom; macular degeneration saw seventy-five degrees when it was actually seventy-three degrees! What a relief! Maintenance left me with the assurance I would be fine in my bedroom with the door shut. After everyone cleared out, I prayed over the dead living room unit, praised God for what He could do with it, set the temp to seventy-three degrees, left my door open, and went to sleep. In the early morning hours, I woke up freezing cold—both units had clicked off at seventy-three degrees! God's protective power had been activated by my prayer of faith, entrusting my Promise Keeper (1 Peter 1:5).

At 11:00 a.m. Saturday morning, my son Bob arrived to escort me across town to one of my favorite restaurants, where forty hearts of love smothered me with bear hugs and sweet kisses. Our special room was so festive with spotlighting on colorful centerpieces of fresh flowers on the tables; they were the perfect prelude to usher in the beautiful testimonies from each guest of our meaningful lifelong relationships as we walked with our precious Lord and Savior. The slideshow presentation Leslie orchestrated by years and themes was incredible! When her equally gifted husband Tony sang "Unforgettable," he turned on our loving tear faucets! For sure, my birthday cake was an original two-tiered surrounded by a circular two-tier white stadium displaying one hundred candles! It took twelve great-grandchildren to help me blow them out! I don't know all the flavors of the extra cakes, but each slice was better than the last! By 5:00 p.m., the last guests had left the party, a few for their short trip to Lake Charles and the others to the motel where those spending the night had been, but Bob and I headed back to the apartment for a short rest before a special foursome came, three grandchildren and their daddy. This was a special time for all of us as we reflected upon and retold the golden memories we treasured with Diane when she was still with us. Some were saturated with tears, but the majority of them were formed with big smiles and hearty laughter.

Sunday morning arrived with a well-organized schedule of twenty-minute "goodbye" slots. With flights to keep, my niece and nephew were the first, and then a grandson and his daughter before their long drive to north Louisiana. In the afternoon, each of the other three grandchildren took their family turns before heading South to the Florida beaches for their annual big family reunion. It was mid-afternoon before silence reigned supreme. That's when this matriarch headed to her throne, pushed back, and drifted off to sleep with unforgettable memories of that incredible celebration of a century.

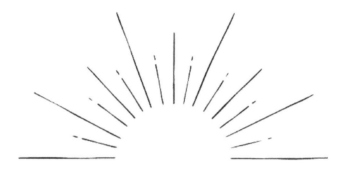

BEACONS OF HOPE

FOR AN

ETERNITY IN HEAVEN

Chapter 25

———◆———

THE LIGHT SWITCH

It had been a delightful fall day at our new R&R place at Toledo Bend Lake: cool in the morning, then warm and sunny by noon. It was like a freshly baked apple pie just out of the oven, crispy on the edges and soft and sweet in the center. Since we had filled the freezer this morning with our large mass of white perch fillets, we decided to skip our trip back to the honey hole and go visit the only other people in the newly opened subdivision whose place was a football field's distance from ours. We had enough time to go, visit a bit outside, and return before night's approach. Because the stroll down the road and the visit outside were so enjoyable, we were easily enticed to hear more "tall tales of whoppers" they caught over a tasty lemonade inside. While the fun time in there had lengthened, the awareness of darkened night skies outside had shortened so suddenly. When we stepped outside, we faced that reality.

The beam from their one lonely light bulb pointed our path of direction, but too quickly vanished back into the eerie black stillness from which it had emerged. The only clue we had that we were on the road was the crunch beneath our faltering feet. We had only empty skies without its usual moon and stars to shine down on the earth; we had only unbuilt houses with their usual friendly lights to encourage our steps; and we had only future dreams of steel lights that would signal our road's direction. All we had was a stone-cold black nothingness and paralyzing fear in panicking hearts. We attempted to move forward inch by inch as we reached upward for help from our loving, all-knowing Father God. He promised He would always listen, and He did not fail us now. Off to our left, way up ahead, we spotted a pinpoint of light. With each step we took, we saw it grow larger. Each time we picked up our pace, it grew faster. When we literally sped in the last lap, our miracle materialized—the light was glowing from our bedroom window on the back of the house that faced the road! Had we gone in there for something before we left and flipped the switch in broad daylight, or did our Heavenly Father meet our need for being Himself? I thank Him for listening and showing us great and mighty things we cannot imagine!

Yes, physical darkness is terrifying, a dreadful experience that seems endless and with no exit signs.

But spiritual darkness is deadly, a destructive condition of a person's soul that is endless and with no exit signs! There is only one exception! A person must choose to: 1.) change his destiny and 2.) turn on the Light!

Turn on the Light

Because this choice of turning on the light switch is everyone's most important life decision, I am going to share the beacons of hope the Lord Jesus gave me. His truth was exactly what I needed.

1. I had to understand I was a sinner, an enemy of the Holy God, and my rebellion against Him was the cause of spiritual darkness. "For all have sinned and fall short of the glory of God" (Romans 3:23). All men, no exclusions. I was a sinner.

2. Because the Holy God is without sin, my sinful condition separated us in what the Bible calls a "death" that is eternal. "For the wages of sin is death, but the gift of God is eternal life in Christ Jesus our Lord" (Romans 6:23).

3. Not wanting me to perish, to live in anguish in hell for eternity, the loving God of the Bible offered me a way of escape from sin's penalty. "For God so loved the world (that's me!) That He gave His only begotten Son, that whosoever believes in Him shall not perish but have everlasting life" (John 3:16). Wonderful words of life!

4. My blessings continued when I read Jesus's words, verifying this truth. "I am the way, the truth, and the light. No one comes to the Father except through Me" (John 14:6). At this point, I had all the head knowledge from God's Word I needed to respond and be reconciled to God. The redemptive story of Jesus on the cross was clear. He had paid my sin debt.

5. When I chose to believe in Jesus, He gave me the next step to take. "If you confess with your mouth the Lord Jesus and believe in your heart that God raised Him from the dead, you will be saved. For with the heart one believes unto righteousness and with the mouth confession is made unto salvation" (Romans 10:9–10).

My destiny for eternity was certain! That special day took place in the sleepy little town of Raymond, Mississippi, when I was twenty-seven years old. That is when I got my name in the Lord's Book of Life. When I became a Christian and when I started living an exciting, abundant life as a child of God.

If you haven't switched on your Light, I trust that these beacons of truth would be exactly what you need to escape your spiritual darkness. Make your most important decision: believe in Jesus, the Source of Light. He will give you a new life of joy, peace, and His perfect goodness. Happy birthday!

The Closing

In the beginning of time, when God created light for the life of His planet, He foreshadowed the brilliant Light of His son Jesus, who would meet the spiritual needs of the people of His planet.

When a man begins his earthly journey, he is not aware of his spiritual darkness. That is why the knowledge of God's truth is essential; God's Word will always convict the human heart. When I began reflecting on my past experiences, writing brief stories, and finding related Scriptures, I did not know my purpose. Only when halfway through the first section did I discover God's purpose. He had woven His Word through the tapestry of all my experiences and made it clear: my experiences were proof of the truth of God's Word. I was to prepare this information in a book to share with others.

For this exciting two-year adventure with the Lord Jesus, I praise Him for directing my steps with His sure and steady beams of light, for dispelling the gloom with His bright rays of joyful sunshine and assuring my destiny in heaven with His bold and blazing beacons of hope. My heartfelt desire for all the readers is that they enjoyed the stories, have been motivated and inspired by the power of God's Word, and have turned on their light switch. Say with me, "Jesus is the Light who is my life."

Milton Keynes UK
Ingram Content Group UK Ltd.
UKHW021815010124
435297UK00016B/883